Compass Points

Horror upon Horror

Researching and Writing
the Horror Novel

Compass Points

Horror upon Horror

Researching and Writing
the Horror Novel

Suzanne Ruthven

**COMPASS
BOOKS**

Winchester, UK
Washington, USA

First published by Compass Books, 2013
Compass Books is an imprint of John Hunt Publishing Ltd., Laurel House, Station Approach,
Alresford, Hants, SO24 9JH, UK
office1@jhpbooks.net
www.johnhuntpublishing.com
www.compass-books.net

For distributor details and how to order please visit the 'Ordering' section on our website.

ISBN: 978 1 78279 266 6

A CIP catalogue record for this book is available from the British Library.

Design: Stuart Davies

Printed and bound by CPI Group (UK) Ltd, Croydon, CR0 4YY

We operate a distinctive and ethical publishing philosophy in all
areas of our business, from our global network of authors to
production and worldwide distribution.

CONTENTS

Chapter One: Tales of the Dead   1

Chapter Two: The Gothic Horror Show   11

Chapter Three: *The Vampyre*   21

Chapter Four: Fakelore and Fantasy   30

Chapter Five: Chimera   45

Chapter Six: The Twilight World   57

Chapter Seven: Nature's Own   67

Cosmic Egg publisher's interview   79

Conclusion   82

Author biography

Suzanne Ruthven is a former member of the now late lamented Gothic Society, a regular contributor to its magazine *Udolpho* during its lifetime, and author of the horror novel, *Whittlewood*. On a more respectable level she is commissioning editor for Compass Books, the writers' resource imprint for John Hunt Publishing. Her latest offering in the horror genre is *House of Strange Gods*, due for publication in 2014.

Chapter One

Tales of the Dead

"The time has come to talk of terror and horror," observed the academic authors of *In Search of Dracula*, Dr Raymond McNally and Professor Radu Florescu. "Strictly speaking they are two different things – but, of course, we seldom speak strictly! Both are responses to the frightful thing, person, deed or circumstance. But terror is the extreme *rational* fear of some accepted form of reality, whereas horror is extreme *irrational* fear of the *utterly* unnatural or the supernatural. Moreover, there is realistic horror – the unnatural or supernatural fright presented in the guise of the normal. Terror is also the dread of the use of systematic violence; horror the dread of something unpredictable, soothing that may have a potential for violence."

In many instances, however, our concept of a favourite horror story comes from a screenplay rather than the original novel, which is a completely different discipline. Many a reader has received a shock when discovering that the novel (often read *after* a cinema or television success), is a drastic departure from the film version. Characters are merged or omitted altogether; locations are altered; new scenes are invented for dramatic impact; and in a large number of cases, the ending is nothing like the novelist's conclusion to the story. Novels are frequently adapted for films and frequently include material that was not part of the original narrative but a film is a film, and a novel is a novel – each being viewed as separate art forms. So, for the time being we must forget about the film versions and concentrate on writing a novel.

To fully understand the horror novel, would-be novelists in the genre are advised to familiarise themselves with the development of the style from the classic German *Gespensterbuch* to the contemporary *Twilight* series, to see what makes the horror novel fan-base tick. The appeal of traditional ghost stories is probably as old as the first time humans gathered together around a fire to listen to tales of long-dead ancestors. The flickering shadows on the walls, the enveloping darkness outside, and the sounds of predatory night creatures would have all added to the atmosphere. A log falling unexpectedly from the flames in a shower of sparks would have sent shivers of fear along the spines of the listeners as they hung on every word ...

... moving down through the ages we come to the famous collection of ghost stories from the Villa Diadoti that inspired the creators of the modern genre. Everyone is familiar with the history:

> *The season was cold and rainy, and in the evenings we crowded around a blazing wood fire, and occasionally amused ourselves with some German stories of ghosts, which happened to fall into our hands. These tales excited in us a playful desire of imitation. Two other friends ... and myself agreed to write a story, founded on some supernatural occurrence ...*

So recorded Percy Shelley in the 'anonymous' preface to the first edition of Mary Shelley's *Frankenstein* in 1818. Mary herself recalled the same collection when she came to write a preface for the revised edition of her novel and although the stories made "so powerful an impression on Mary Shelley that she could recall incidents which occurred in them fifteen years later, no-one has until now thought fit to reprint either the French or the English editions," observed Dr Terry Hale of the Performance Translation Centre at the University of Hull, in the 1992 translation published by the Gothic Society.

The original German collection, *Gespensterbuch*, first saw the light of day between 1811 and 1815, with the French version, *Fantasmagoriana* published in 1812; and an English version, *Tales of the Dead*, appearing the following year. These German 'shudder' stories had a tremendous influence on the development of the English Gothic literary genre and according to Dr Hale, "frequently employed traditional folk-motifs coupled with increasingly sophisticated narrative techniques". A technique that is still highly identifiable in the genre in the twentieth century – but from that 'wet, ungenial summer' also sprung the independent trains of thought that gave the world two of its most terrifying Gothic creations – Dr Frankenstein's monster and, subsequently, the charismatic vampire, Count Dracula.

The traditional ghost story, however, is usually based on some form of revenge or retribution from beyond the grave, and whereas contemporary writers have moved on from the classical 'moaning in the passages' and 'clanking chains', the narrative must still produce that involuntary 'shudder factor' in the reader. It is a scenario that bridges generations, just as the 1898 novella, *The Turn of the Screw* by Henry James partly inspired the screenplay for the psychological horror film *The Others* (2001). It is also the one of the most 'respectable' elements of the horror genre in that ghost stories have graced the pages of the most surprising of mainstream magazines at one time or another, including an edition of *Practical Fishkeeping*!

By definition, however, a ghost story should be any piece of fiction, ballad or drama, or an account of an experience, that includes a ghost, or simply has all the appearances of a haunting. Wikipedia, for example, tells us: "In a narrower sense, the ghost story has been developed as a short story format, within genre fiction. It is a form of supernatural fiction and specifically of weird fiction, and is often a horror story. While ghost stories are often explicitly meant to be scary, they have been written to serve all sorts of purposes, from comedy to morality tales. Ghosts often appear in the narrative as sentinels or prophets of things to come. Whatever their uses the ghost story is in some format present in all cultures around the world, and may be passed down orally or in written form."

Literary scholar and historian of the ghost story Jack Sullivan, observes that many literary experts claim a 'Golden Age of the Ghost Story' existed between the decline of the Gothic novel in the 1830s and the start of the First World War. Sullivan's opinion is that the work of Edgar Allan Poe and Sheridan Le Fanu ushered in the 'Golden Age' – but fails to acknowledge Arthur Machen's contribution to the genre, especially his ghostly tale of *The Bowmen*, that actually inspired the WWI legend of the Angels of Mons. Sullivan is one of the leading modern figures in the study of the horror genre, particularly the ghost story, and probably his most important contribution to the historical study of the genre to date has been the mammoth *The Penguin Encyclopaedia of Horror and the Supernatural*, which should be on every horror writer's bookshelf.

Nevertheless every location on earth has its ghost story to tell, its haunted house, local superstition or folklore that can be drawn upon to enrich a fictional tale, from Shakespeare's *Hamlet* (1603), to Sir Arthur Conan Doyle's *The Hound of the Baskervilles* (1902) – which was listed on the BBC's 'The Big Read' poll as the 'UK's best-loved novel' – and *The Amityville Horror*, an American best-selling novel (1977) by Jay Anson. On a more personal and factual front, Passenham Manor in Buckinghamshire has its own 'Bobby' Bannister whose memory is preserved as 'an oppressive tyrant whose ghost still lingers on,' (*Passenham: A History of a Forest Village*), having broken his neck in the hunting field and the horse dragging his mangled body home.

Perhaps the longest running ghost story theme, using the idea of ancestral haunting, is the animated portrait … first introduced in *The Castle of Otranto* by Horace Walpole in 1764. Generally regarded as the first Gothic novel and a major literary influence for Charles Maturin, Ann Radcliffe, Bram Stoker and Edgar Allan Poe, the author uses the device of "the portrait of his grandfather which hung over the bench where they had been sitting uttered a deep sigh and heaved its breast ..." thus preventing a ravishment that while not incestuous was certainly on the borderland of consanguinity.

As Terry Hale observes: "Animated portraits became a familiar stock-in-trade of the Gothic novel throughout the 1790s. Maturin was responsible for the most artistically successful use of the motif in his *Melmoth the Wanderer* (1820). When Melmoth burns the painting of his ancestor as demanded by his uncle's will, 'its undulations gave the portrait the appearance of smiling' as the wrinkled and torn canvas fell to the ground ... this motif would re-emerge seventy years later in Wilde's *Dorian Gray* ..." While 'The Family Portraits' in *Tales of the Dead* bears a marked similarity to one of those related by Mathew Gregory Lewis – the author of *The Monk* – when he visited Lord Byron's house party at the Villa Diodoti in August 1816, and which was jotted down by Percy Shelley in the diary he shared with his sister.

The acknowledged master of the ghost story, however, is still M R James, English medieval scholar and provost of King's College, Cambridge and Eton. James drew on his own antiquarian interests to flesh out his protagonists and plots, and redefined the ghost story for the twentieth century by abandoning many of the formal Gothic clichés of his predecessors by using more realistic contemporary settings. The narrative usually included three main ingredients:

- an atmospheric village, seaside town or country estate; an ancient town, abbey or university;
- a rather vague and naive academic as protagonist;
- the discovery of a book or antiquarian object that summons up, calls down, or attracts the unwelcome attention of a supernatural agency, usually from beyond the grave.

He added this advice for would-be 'ghost' writers: "Another

requisite, in my opinion, is that the ghost should be malevolent or odious: amiable and helpful apparitions are all very well in fairy tales or in local legends, but I have no use for them in a fictitious ghost story." And: "Two ingredients most valuable in the concocting of a ghost story are, to me, the atmosphere and the nicely managed crescendo ... Let us, then, be introduced to the actors in a placid way; let us see them going about their ordinary business, undisturbed by forebodings, pleased with their surroundings; and into this calm environment let the ominous thing put out its head, unobtrusively at first, and then more insistently, until it holds the stage."

The scholarly narrative should not for one moment suggest that James's writing is too bland for the palette of today's horror genre. Many of his tales depict scenes and images of savage and often disturbing violence: for example, in *Lost Hearts*, adolescent children fall victim to a sinister dabbler in the occult who cuts their hearts from their still-living bodies! He wrote: "Malevolence and terror, the glare of evil faces, 'the stony grin of unearthly malice', pursuing forms in darkness, and 'long-drawn, distant screams', are all in place, and so is a modicum of blood, shed with deliberation and carefully husbanded; the weltering and wallowing that I too often encounter merely recall the methods of M G Lewis ['Monk' Lewis]."

In addition to writing his own stories, James championed the works of Sheridan Le Fanu, whom he viewed as "absolutely in the first rank as a writer of ghost stories", editing and supplying introductions to *Madame Crowl's Ghost* (1923) and *Uncle Silas* (1926).

The contemporary 'ghost' story involves the manifestation of the 'undead' interacting with the physical world as opposed to the vampire, who retains a *parasitic dependency* on its human victims. When writing my own horror novel, *Whittlewood*, the 'undead' protagonist was a Celtic shaman who had returned to avenge the defilement of an ancient burial site. He had no physical form but his magical abilities had been so powerful in life that he was capable of producing a simulacrum, or 'thought form' to do his bidding almost 2000 years after his death.

Haunted houses, however, have provided the contemporary horror writer – and the film companies – with licence for the most amazing visual and special effects. The prerequisite for success is an abandoned mansion set in a remote location, with some disgruntled ghost that vents its psychic spleen on some unsuspecting family, who usually have no responsibility for the reasons behind the disturbances. The most famous novel in this genre is *The Haunting of Hill House* by Shirley Jackson (1959) – finalist for the National Book Award and considered one of the best literary ghost stories published during the twentieth century, which has been made into two feature films and a play. "Jackson relies on terror rather than horror to elicit emotion by the reader, utilizing complex relationships between the mysterious events in the house and the characters' psyches."

By comparison, *Hell House* (1971) by American novelist Richard Matheson, relies on pure horror and although the novel has marked similarities to Jackson's, the narrative is shot through with much more violence and sexual imagery. Stephen King's *The Shining* (1977) used the setting of a remote, out-of-season hotel and established him as the pre-eminent author in the horror genre. A film based upon the book, directed by Stanley Kubrick and starring Jack Nicholson, was released in 1980, and later adapted into a TV mini-series in 1997.

Another literary element of the 'undead' (and often in conjunction with the haunted house scenario) is the result of a long-forgotten curse or psychic infestation that often involves small children, often themselves the grisly perpetrators of unspeakable horror. This device is also employed in historical horror fiction since history is littered with ancient curses; or a contemporary story with its roots in the dim and distant past.

Anyone contemplating writing horror stories can gain an

immeasurable wealth of knowledge concerning techniques and narrative style from these acknowledged 'greats' in the genre. We may decide to try our hand at short stories in the M R James mould; or we may prefer to embark straightaway on the novel – but whichever way we decide to go, there are still the preliminaries of learning how to pace the injections of horror into the narrative to create the best effect on the reader.

Without a doubt, the technique and narrative style of *Tales of the Dead* and *In A Glass Darkly* do appear extremely dated by today's literary standards but as with all aspects of creative writing, it is always a good idea to have a thorough grounding in the development of the genre before committing our own words to paper – and to be constantly aware that we are still looking to create that **extreme irrational fear of the utterly unnatural or the supernatural** in our writing.

Ideas and Inspiration

Ghost stories come from all over the globe, so we are not restricted to home-grown hauntings. We can, in fact, utilise almost any supernatural presence in any location, providing that we've done our homework and can give a fairly credible account of the antecedents of the ritual, artefact, text, etc., that has unleashed your 'horror' into the world. In other words, there has to be someone among the *dramatis personae* capable of identifying and dealing with the problem convincingly. Bram Stoker's *The Jewel of the Seven Stars* is an excellent, classic example. Perhaps we should also bear in mind M R James's observation that 'ghosts' in horror stories should be "malevolent or odious" as opposed to the "amiable and helpful apparitions" of fairy tales is still applicable to modern writing.

Exercise

For the first exercise we turn to Krystina Kellingley, publisher of Cosmic Egg, a John Hunt Publishing imprint that specialises

in science fiction, fantasy and horror novels. This extract first appeared on the Cosmic Egg blog as a guide for potential horror writers:

> The first thing to do is to think about what kinds of horror novels you like reading. Having done that the next question is to ask yourself: why? What is it about these particular novels that stand out against others that you didn't enjoy quite as much?
>
> Now sit down and make a list. Was it the plot? If you answered yes to this then now is the time to break it down more fully for yourself. Which elements of the plot had you particularly gripped? What else made you keep on reading and held your rapt attention? Were the characters believable? Did you care about them and what happened to them? Was there lots of tension to keep you turning pages? Perhaps there was also a burgeoning romance with lots of conflict thrown in for good measure? Was the pacing tight? The dialogue snappy? Did you, the reader, know something that the characters weren't yet aware of? What didn't you like?

Lots of questions here but all equally valid if you want to understand exactly what kind of horror novel *you* want to write. Analysing the influence of your favourites, may help you to avoid running out of steam half way through, or the mistake of cross-threading the structure of the plot without realising it. (see Chapter Five: Chimera)

and check out the Horror Writers' Association

HWA is a non-profit organisation of writers and publishing professionals around the world, dedicated to promoting dark literature and the interests of those who write it. HWA was formed in the late 1980s with the help of many of the field's greats, including Dean Koontz, Robert McCammon, and Joe

Lansdale. "Today, with over 800 members around the globe, it is the oldest and most respected professional organization for the much-loved writers who have brought you the most enjoyable sleepless nights of your life."

http://www.horror.org

Chapter Two

The Gothic Horror Show

Gothic fiction, often referred to as 'Gothic horror', is a branch of literature that juxtaposes the elements of both horror *and* romance, with its origins attributed to Horace Walpole's novel *The Castle of Otranto* (1764), subtitled 'A Gothic Story'. Or as *Udolpho* magazine's contributor Denis Moss uncharitably explained: "The ingredients of these eighteenth-century thrillers do not vary very much – the heroine is young, beautiful, unprotected, aristocratic, well-educated, musical, artistic and, at the end of the novel at least, a wealthy heiress about to marry a wealthy young man. There is usually a half-ruined castle or monastery, some lost treasure, remote but romantic scenery, some loyal medieval-type servants who know their place, and supernatural happenings which turn out to have a prosaic explanation."

Employing all these ingredients, Anne Radcliffe became the 'premier Gothicist' of her time by using a technique of giving the reasoning behind the 'inexplicable phenomena' in her final revelations, which of course gave an aura of 1790s respectability to her novels. Further contributions to the Gothic genre were provided by Percy Bysshe Shelley's Gothic novel *Zastrozzi* (1810), about an outlaw obsessed with revenge against his father and half-brother, and another published in 1811, *The Rosicrucian* (or *St. Irvyne*) about an alchemist who seeks to impart the secret of immortality.

The real clincher for the Gothic novel, however were the real life romantic adventures and character of Lord Byron – characterised by his spurned mistress Lady Caroline Lamb as 'mad, bad and dangerous to know' – and the inspiration behind every archetype of the Byronic hero. George, Lord Byron features under the codename of 'Lord Ruthven', in Lady Caroline's own Gothic offering, *Glenarvon* (1816) and that this was common knowledge is reflected in J C Hobhouse's record: "Yesterday Lady Caroline Lamb published a novel, *Glenarvon*. The hero is a monster, and meant for Byron."

> That which was disgusting or terrific to man's nature had no power over Glenarvon. He had looked upon the dying and the dead had seen the tear of agony without emotion; had heard the shriek of despair, and felt the hot blood as it flowed from the heart of a murdered enemy, not turned from the sickening sight ... [*Lord Byron*, Joanna Richardson]

A late example of traditional Gothic is *Melmoth the Wanderer* 1820) by Charles Maturin, which combines themes of anti-Catholicism with yet another outcast Byronic hero. And, of course, no collection would be complete without reference to Mary Shelley's own tragic *Frankenstein* (the first edition published anonymously in London in 1818. Shelley's name appears on the second edition, published in France in 1823); Elizabeth Gaskell's tales (1858) all full of ancestral sins to curse future generations; and the gloomy villain, forbidding mansion, and persecuted heroine of Sheridan Le Fanu's *Uncle Silas* (1864) shows the direct influence of both Walpole's *Otranto* and Radcliffe's *Udolpho*.

For authentic, unspeakable Gothic horror of the period, however, we cannot ignore *The Monk* by Matthew Lewis (1796) and by sadistic standards, it even won the approval of 'the divine Marquise'. The novel has been 'attacked, praised, held in contempt, and examined as a literary curio' for over two centuries but its numerous editions, several chapbook versions and paperbacks have ensured that it didn't pass into oblivion, according to D P Varma of Dalhousie University.

The rape of Antonia alongside the 'three putrid half-corrupted bodies' has a horrifying sadistic touch. The entire setting, 'the gloom of the vault, the surrounding silence, and the resistance which he [Ambrosio the monk] expected from her seemed to give a fresh edge to his fierce and unbridled desires ... The prolonged gory description of Ambrosio's death, with detailed focus upon his sufferings, deleted from subsequent editions, smacks of the manner of de Sade.

Nevertheless, the genre continued to influence more mainstream writers, such as Charles Dickens, who read Gothic novels as a teenager and incorporated their gloomy atmosphere and melodrama into his own works, shifting them to a more modern period and an urban setting, including *Oliver Twist* (1837-8), *Bleak House* (1854) and *Great Expectations* (1860–61). Here was juxtaposition of wealthy, ordered and affluent civilisation within the same metropolis as the disorder and barbarity of the poor. Victorian London was notorious for its thick smogs, or 'pea-soupers', and often used to created an air of mystery to period drama; *Bleak House* in particular is credited with the introduction of urban fog to the novel, which would become an often used characteristic of urban Gothic literature and film.

The gloomy ambiance and macabre themes of the genre held a particular fascination for the Victorians, with their obsession with mourning rituals, *memento mori*, and mortality in general. Classic works of this revival include Robert Louis Stevenson's *Strange Case of Dr Jekyll and Mr Hyde* (1886); Oscar Wilde's *The Picture of Dorian Gray* (1891); George du Maurier's *Trilby* (1894); Henry James's *The Turn of the Screw* (1898) and Gaston Leroux's *The Phantom of the Opera* (1909–1910).

Despite a national penchant for the ghostly and macabre, Arthur Machen remains one of the world's most sadly neglected writers. Although his works are in many ways superior to his American counterpart, Edgar Allan Poe, Machen has remained a virtual unknown – even a contemporary volume of *Masters of the Macabre* omits his name from the hallowed ranks of literary horror, and modern writers in the genre remain unaware of his genius. His controversial *The Great God Pan* was published in 1894, and the novel relates the story of a diabolical medical experiment performed on a servant-girl by her employer. The result of which is a fiendish girl-child who grows into a beautiful but deadly monster. Critics of the time denounced the work as 'repulsive', 'ludicrous' and 'gruesome', but fired by the unexpected furore the novel had created, Machen set out to create a collection of superbly told stories of 'mysticism and ancient evil'.

He was one of the first writes of the horror genre to realise that hinting at diabolical evil was more effective than explicit description. As his co-biographer Roger Dobson suggests, his style may have been influenced by the way that the sins of Hyde and Dorian Grey were never clearly defined by their creators, "leaving the reader to conjure up his own visions of evil". Machen's stories of mystery and ancient evil, inspired by the landscape and pagan rites of his Welsh homeland, nevertheless profoundly influenced later writers in the genre, including H P Lovecraft and the *Weird Tales* circle. Jerome K Jerome wrote: "For ability to create an atmosphere of nameless terror I can think of no author living or dead who comes near him."

One of the greatest contemporary exponents of these literary devices was the late Simon Raven, who was described as having "the mind of a cad and the pen of an angel". His unashamed credo was "a robust eighteenth-century paganism ..." and his cruel delight in the outrageous, and lack of moralising or sentiment, are characteristics which pervade his writings. He also had a marked fascination for the supernatural, first manifested in an early novel *Doctors Wear Scarlet* (1960), which features vampirism as a sexual deviation rather than an actual supernatural manifestation. This novel was cited by Karl Edward

Wagner – himself an award-winning American writer, poet, editor and publisher of horror and writer of numerous dark fantasy and horror stories – as one of the thirteen best super-natural novels of all time. These Gothic themes became stronger in Raven's later works such as *The Roses of Picardie* (1980), *September Castle* (1983), parts of the *First-Born of Egypt* series, and his last 1994 novella *The Islands of Sorrow*.

The one over-riding feature of all these literary works was that they were penned by men and women of letters, who used their command of the English language to weave a web of horror, without saying anything out of place. It might be described dismissively today as 'purple prose' but that's what makes the classic 'horror' stand out from most contemporary novels; that and the ability to create the hint of diabolical evil and an atmos-phere of nameless horror rather than explicit description – **the unnatural or supernatural fright presented in the guise of the normal**.

Ideas and Inspiration

Modern Gothic still requires the elements of horror and romance, although it is difficult to combine these essential ingredients in a way that appeal to the contemporary publisher without resorting to a nineteenth-century scenario. The secret is to be able to use all the traditional trademarks of classic Gothic within a modern narrative and/or theme. A good example of this sub-genre is Simon Raven's *September Castle,* a strange tale that manages to utilise the beautiful, aristocratic heroine (albeit deceased), together with the obligatory half-ruined castle, loyal medieval-type servants and plenty of supernatural happenings to satisfy even the most demanding modern reader. Although not a novel, *Midnight in the Garden of Good and Evil* by John Berendt, contains a lot of elements that could be described as a 'Southern Gothic' background with its crumbling Savannah mansions, old families and lashings of Santeria to help move the narrative along in this unique writing style of dressing up fact as fiction.

Session 1: Who's going to read my novel?

The first question I ask every workshop participant and one that every potential novelist should ask themselves, is: **Who is going to read my novel?** Every target market for consumable products is subject to marketing analysis by the producer. The fact that we are talking about books (the horror genre in particular), and publishers, doesn't alter the fact that we are still referring to a commodity that will be aimed at a particular target market (i.e. readership). So we must start by identifying the type of reader for whom we are telling our story.

At this stage, someone will always interrupt and complain that this is not a creative approach to novel writing; or that they found this idea inhibiting, strangling the creative urge at birth; or even that they are writing for themselves and are not bothered about who will read the finished story.

Unfortunately, there are still the last shreds of glamour clinging to the image of the novelist and up to twenty years ago we could still allow ourselves the luxury of not compromising our personal integrity by becoming a slave to commercialism. A couple of decades down the road, publishing is the sole province of the accountants and *every* book is looked upon in terms of profit and loss – not literary merit. And so the truly ambitious make a point of understanding who's publishing what in today's book world.

The next interruption usually voices the opinion that no one told the 'greats' (Le Fanu, Radcliffe, *et al.*) how to write; not taking into account that the 'greats' wouldn't get past the first glance by today's publisher's reader. Take my own personal favourites, whom I still read repeatedly for pleasure – Balzac and Arthur Machen. Poor old Arthur and Honoré, with their 'tell don't show' technique would have been blue-pencilled into oblivion, despite the fact that their work inspired many later writers.

So the image we have to dispel is the vision of the by-gone literary world of Radcliffe, Stoker, Le Fanu, Poe, Maturin, Wilde and Lewis (to name a few more favourites) when publishers and agents appreciated a good use of the English language, and knuckle down to the fact that we are competing in a vast commercial process of producing a book that might only have a few weeks of modest fame on the shelves of Waterstones or Tescos; or being remaindered and never heard of again! This is the reality of contemporary publishing and what we hope to do during these exercises is attempt to narrow the odds a little in the outsider's favour ...

The first thing we need to establish is identifying the sub-genre in which we are writing ... so-called 'slip stream' or 'cross genre' novels are fun to write but infinitely more difficult to sell, so a lot of deliberation needs to go into this answer. Broadly speaking, the most popular commercial horror novels fit into the following categories:

- The ghost story: haunted houses and returns from the dead – especially children.
- Neo-Gothic: anything with a period flavour that uses historical devices coupled with romance for effect.
- Vampire tales: updated vampire stories, such as *Twilight* and *Vampire Dairies.*
- Fakelore and fantasy: creatures from the Abyss, loosely based on a pseudo-ritual magic scenario and possibly more thriller than horror.
- Cross genre: the blending of traditional horror techniques with, for example, science fiction, history or crime.
- Mind games: psychological chillers that move out of the realm of crime/detection into the hunter and the hunted.
- Animals: killer animals on the rampage.

There will be other sub-genres that still manage to produce the odd rabbit out of the hat, but these days publishers tend to stick with tried and tested authors, rather than taking on new ones in an untried area. There is also the 'literary' Gothic sub-genre that might be reflected in the type of writing that could be chosen for a Booker shortlist, or new novels from the graduates of the University of East Anglia. This is, of course, a very general overview of modern publishing but the odds-on favourite for new authors will be those who *don't* try to invent a sub-genre with a built-in marketing problem.

The second step in the exercise is to identify your own target readership, because at the end of the day, this will make it easier to target the *right* agent or publisher for the finished typescript. What type of person would you generally expect to pick up your novel from the shelves of a high street bookshop? This is the same kind of market research we do when first starting writing and we learn to identify the readership of a certain type of magazine or newspaper. It is also applicable to marketing a genre novel, and we learn to keep an eye open in bookshops for the latest releases, especially those similar to our own intended plot and/or theme.

Just as we select the right target market for an article or short story, so we learn to make sure that our typescript is targeted at the right area of publishing ... there is no magical formula for this, just plain common sense. You are a potential novelist and have to supply what the publisher wants. As Chriss McCallum writes in *The Writers' Guide to Getting Published,* "You are the manufacturer, and you have to supply what the retailer wants. An editor is a retailer. He buys from the manufacturer – the writer – what he knows he can sell to his customers – his readers – or in this case, the book buying public."

So, this is no time to be precious. Get to understand the current horror marketplace but just for starters, here are a few 'rules' that you would do well to take on board:

- Don't try to ride on the tail of what's currently in fashion – by the time your novel is finished, never mind the time it takes between contract and launch – it will be outdated.

- Don't bore the reader. Can your story retain the reader's interest for 80,000 words?

- Don't try to base an entire horror novel on a single fragment of an idea. It may be a brilliant opening or closing scene, but without a detailed structure to unite ideas, characters, setting, drama, tension, plot and action, it *will* be extremely difficult to maintain the momentum.

- Don't get disheartened.

To return to the original question at the start of this piece and before doing anything else, let us identify our target reader. Few contemporary horror novels cover the whole spectrum of age, gender and literary style. Books written by younger authors tend to reflect the viewpoints of their own generation, although mature authors often appeal to much younger readers, as well as the older generation. Secondly, gratuitous sex and/or violence will have its own following and the writer must be able to differentiate between the requirements of the various publishers, so be prepared to spend some time in your local bookstore and find out who publishes what.

Thirdly, let's try to establish who or what the novel is about. Most horror novels are plot-driven, rather than character-driven – and to help us clarify which path we intend to take, it is a good idea to write a short 'blurb' for the story. In the publishing trade this is understood to be the short precise of the story, and examples can be found on the back cover of most paperback books. Try to précis your novel in around 150 words to show whether the emphasis is on a human-interest story, action/horror packed chiller, adventure, etc. and record the answers to all the exercises in a special notebook for future reference and comparison notes.

Exercise: Session 1 – Who's going to read my novel?

1. Prepare a synopsis for the novel.
2. Describe your target market/sub-genre where you think your finished typescript will be aimed.
3. Describe your target readership in terms of who you think will enjoy your book.
4. Which publishers have novels similar in approach to your own on their titles list?
5. Prepare a 'blurb' in no more than 150 words to show the outline for the story.
6. Prepare main character biographies for your two principal characters in less than 50 words for each.
7. Identify where *you* feel the novel could run out of steam.

and check out Goodreads online

Goodreads claims to be the world's largest free website for book lovers and book recommendations. Surprisingly, in the Popular Horror Fiction category the top three ratings are *The Shining* (Stephen King), *Interview with the Vampire* (Ann Rice) and *Salem's Lot* (Stephen King), with *Dracula* (Bram Stoker) in sixth place. "Imagine it as a large library that you can wander through and see everyone's bookshelves, their reviews, and their ratings. You can also post your own reviews and catalog what you have read, are currently reading, and plan to read in the future. Don't stop there – join a discussion group, start a book club, contact an author, and even post your own writing. Signing up is simple – you just enter your name, email, and a password."

www.goodreads.com

Chapter Three

The Vampyre

And it started with a kiss – or rather a wet summer of debauchery and the challenge to create a modern 'ghost story'. As a result *The Vampyre*, although written by John William Polidori, first appeared in April 1819 under Lord Byron's name in the *New Monthly Magazine*. *The Vampyre* has been accounted by cultural critic Christopher Frayling as one of the most influential works of fiction ever written and spawned a craze for vampire fiction and theatre (and latterly film) which has not ceased to this day.

The first instalment of the penny novel, *Varney the Vampire*, or the *Feast of Blood* by Thomas Preskett Prest, appeared in 1847 – a very popular Gothic horror story in which a well-educated, gentleman-vampire, Sir Francis Varney, plagues the Bannerworth family. In the novelette, *Carmilla*, Joseph Sheridan Le Fanu created the most famous female vampire in English literature, and it was this masterpiece of Gothic horror that inspired Bram Stoker to write a vampire story of his own. According to McNally-Florescu (*In Search of Dracula*) "if one could read only one piece of vampire fiction, this should be it." – Bram Stoker's *Dracula*.

There are certain elements of vampire-lore, however, that the writer ignores at their peril. For example: an apotropaic, is an amulet worn to ward off an attack by a revenant, or vampire, and occurs in all folklore – garlic being the most common in literature, although the rarely used wood from the wild rose and hawthorn has the same affect. Other amulets include any sacred items such as a crucifix, rosary, bible or holy water – unless your vampire happens to be Jewish as in the case of Roman Polanski's film *Dance of the Vampires* (1967: or *The Fearless Vampire Killers* in the USA.)

Despite the methods of repelling a vampire being relatively simple, the actual methods of their destruction are numerous, complicated and the more time-consuming the better, from the novelist's point of view. The most frequently cited is to drive a wooden stake through the creature's heart, usually ash or hawthorn, or sometimes oak, depending on the location and according to local tradition. There are variations using metal implements instead of wood – which were interred with the corpse at the time of burial. A vampire could also be killed by being shot (silver bullet optional); by being drowned in running water; or the sprinkling of holy water on the body.

Decapitation featured strongly, with the head buried between the feet, behind the buttocks, or away from the body. If the body were not burned then the head, body or clothes should be pinned to the earth to prevent the vampire from getting out of the grave. In some cases the body was dismembered, the pieces burned and the ashes scattered into fast flowing water. Alternatives to a stake through the heart was the use of a consecrated dagger (which was used to despatch Dracula), or consecrated silver bullets. A vampire should only be struck once or it will reanimate; and care should be taken not to expose a vampire's body to moonlight, as this will also restore it. Surprisingly, the latter was ignored by Stoker in his novel, while Sir Francis Varney was restored by this method having been shot by Flora Bannerworth. Carmilla was dealt with in the traditional manner but Lord Ruthven, however, got away with murder!

There have, of course, been numerous vampire novels since the literary classics and the most outstanding are those that retain traditional vampire lore, but choose unusual and uncharacteristic settings for the story to give it an original slant. For example, *Doctors Wear Scarlet* (1960) by Simon Raven used the backdrop of Cambridge University and the Aegean islands for his Greek vampire. The action of *The Vampires of Alfama* (1975) by Pierre

Kast takes place in a medieval ghetto in eighteenth-century Lisbon. Louise Cooper for *Blood Summer* (1976) used a Cornish setting for the introduction to her vampire, who was himself the victim of an ancient curse; while in same year, *Interview with the Vampire* by Anne Rice, moved the action to Louisiana. *The Hunger* (1983) by Whitley Strieber in stark contrast offers a highly influential, modernised and urbanised version of vampire culture; while *The Vampire Diaries* (1991) by L J Smith introduced a young adult vampire horror series of novels for a new generation readership. *The Merciful Women* (1998) by Federico Andahazi turned the clock back to the Villa Diodati in 1816 for a very different kind of vampirism for adults – with the *Twilight* (2005) series of vampire-themed fantasy romance novels by American author Stephenie Meyer providing the latest teenage offering to gain worldwide recognition and selling over 100 million copies, with translations into 37 different languages ...

With its continuing and **extreme irrational fear of the utterly unnatural or the supernatural**, who says the vampire-cult is dead?

Ideas and Inspiration

The vampire theme has undergone many transformations although the basic vampire-lore remains constant, in that the creatures have a parasitic dependence on human energy sources to survive.

And since the concept of the vampire exists in every culture and creed, the writer has an enormous wealth of locations and plots to drawn upon. For *Interview with the Vampire*, Anne Rice drew on the Deep South; Colin Wilson's *Space Vampires* were intergalactic aliens; Pierre Kast's *The Vampires of Alfama* existed in an eighteenth-century fantasy world; Simon Raven's vampire in *Doctors Wear Scarlet* was Greek; Stephen King used small town America for *Salem's Lot*; while Louise Cooper's vampire resurrected an ancient curse from Ninevah in *Blood Summer*. From adult erotica to teenage fantasy, providing the 'facts' are right, the writer has free rein over his/her own imagination.

Session 2: Theme, Plot and Structure

The main reason why most first novels flounder, is usually the lack of planning and preparation *before* the writer gets down to the serious work. In the first session we looked at identifying the readership and publishers likely to be interested in your horror novel, and the 150 word 'blurb' will have given the outline of the plot but now we need to take the next step forward.

Theme:

The 'theme' gives the story its tone, its subject matter, its 'reader identity/empathy' and can often be summed up in a single word: jealousy, revenge, ambition, deliverance, self-discovery, flight, fight, etc. The theme is the core of the story – the plot development can be thought of as layers of an onion. The Polti theory maintains that there are only 36 dramatic situations on which the writer of fiction can draw. By using single situations or several combinations, the basic theme of every horror story (long or short) ever told, written, filmed or devised, can be summed up in the following list:

Supplication: Deliverance: Crime pursued by vengeance: Vengeance taken for kindred upon kindred: Pursuit: Disaster: Falling prey to cruelty or misfortune: Revolt: Daring Enterprise: Abduction: The Enigma: Obtaining: Enmity of kinsmen: Rivalry of kinsmen: Murderous adultery: Madness: Fatal imprudence: Involuntary crimes of love: Slaying of a kinsman unrecognised: Self sacrifice for an ideal: Self sacrifice for kindred: All sacrificed for passion: Necessity of sacrificing loved ones: Rivalry of superior and inferior: Adultery: Crimes of love: Discovery of the dishonour of a loved one: Obstacles to love: An enemy loved: Ambition: Conflict with God: Mistaken jealousy: Erroneous judgement: Remorse: Recovery of a lost one: Loss of a loved one.

For the horror novel to work, the reader *must* be convinced that the principal character has good reason/motivation/ability to follow the course of action needed to carry the plot along. Simply, if the principal character is unconvincing, no amount of clever plotting will compensate for that lack of credibility, because readers identify with the course of action and if it doesn't convince them that *they* would act in the same manner, the interest will be lost.

Plot and Sub-Plot:

The 'plot' refers to the storyline that drives the characters into behaving the way they do and is concerned with precisely how the theme is put into effect. And the first question we should ask ourselves is: **Will the story be strong enough to hold the reader's attention for 80,000+ words?** It is pointless starting with a good idea for an opening and not giving any further thought to how the story will develop – travelling hopefully is not the best way to begin a novel!

Regardless of the type of story we are writing, there needs to be plenty of tension and drama – particularly for the horror genre. These elements provide the barriers and obstacles that everyone must overcome in order to resolve the 'problem' that is at the root of the plot. They are also useful tools to provide the antagonism between the various characters because drama does not arrive in a story unbidden ... something has to create it and the reader must be convinced by it. The 'horror' cannot arrive fully-fledged without there being some form of explanation for it manifesting when it does. We must clearly work out **what** it is; **where** it comes from; **why** it has suddenly emerged; **when** it first appeared and **how** it has been brought into being.

Another point to consider at this stage is that very few novels are able to sustain reader interest without there being some form of sub-plot. This can be a mystery/misunderstanding running parallel to the main plot; it can be developed to involve one of the other characters while only superficially imposing on the storyline; it can provide a useful red herring; it can be anything you like providing it adds breadth and dimension to your story.

The plot will also be governed by the time span of the story and it is a good idea to decide, right from the start, when the story will begin and end. We all know that a story should begin with a point of high drama in order to hook the reader's attention but for how long a period of time are we going to spin the story out? If the story is planned to unfold in, say, the period of a week, then all the necessary background information can be revealed by means of conversation or flashback, rather than in some extended introduction.

According to publisher Krystina Kellingley, one of the most common mistakes new writers make is to start the story too late:

> There is no time to waste in a slow build up as you introduce your characters and unravel your story. Start with the action. Make your first sentence strong; the first paragraph equally strong and the first five pages even stronger. If you can succeed in accomplishing this then you will have hooked your reader. Start with something **BIG** happening. An attack, physical or psychic or a murder; an occult ritual or séance where something goes badly wrong; the horrendous beastie entering into the world, bedroom, life of a character (even if this character is minor and is about to meet their demise).

This time element can be an extremely useful device in creating drama because the characters come to the action primed and ready to participate. It plunges the reader straight into the action and any relevant background details can be introduced later by using various different techniques.

Structure:

Whether a horror novel is character or plot-driven, the setting we choose for the story *must* play an integral part. The setting provides a backdrop against which the story takes place, while painting a visual picture and adding authenticity: without a credible setting, the characters would be acting out their parts on a bare stage. Exotic and/or original locations can give a story an extra boost. As we have seen, Anne Rice began *Interview with the Vampire* on a plantation in Louisiana; while Simon Raven utilised Cambridge University and various historical sites in France, Greece and Italy for *Roses of Picardy, September Castle, Islands of Sorrow* and *Doctors Wear Scarlet*.

Having a firm idea of where the novel is set will help considerably when it comes down to structuring a provisional mind map of chapters and action because the setting will help to dictate where (and often when) the action takes place. Novelists have all sorts of methods of structuring a novel – some use blank cards, other use computer spreadsheets, some even use lining paper from the DIY store. It really doesn't matter because we all approach novel writing in different ways, so find something with which you feel comfortable and start planning.

Study contemporary horror novels in the same sub-genre to gauge the number of chapters you should be aiming for. For example, some like my own *Whittlewood*, may run to 24+ long chapters because of the constant shift of perception and viewpoint; while a more localised and contained story like Federico Andahazi's *The Merciful Women* contained 30+ short chapters.

The initial choice for the number of chapters isn't cast in stone but it does give a firm starting point on which to structure the complete novel. If we go for the short time span, there needs to be a lot happening in a short space of time; a wide time span will need to be carefully divided so that the story doesn't become unevenly time-bound in one period. Start with a card or separate sheet for each chapter and begin to map out the point of introduction of your characters and the relevant action involving each of them. Don't worry too much if they start to take on a life of their own, this is normal and often produces some interesting results.

Remember that structure is merely a guide to show where the story needs its peaks and troughs. All novels (even horror) have the occasional slow periods, to allow the reader to catch their breath before charging off for another piece of action.

For commissioning editor appeal, *all* fiction needs a credible plot, a plausible theme, an original location and principal characters who, whilst being sharp, intelligent and 'successful', need to possess a few faults and foibles to give them added dimension. At my 'Kick-Starting the Novel' workshops, the most frequent comment in response to all this advice, is that the participants sometimes feel such preparation to be stifling the creative urge of writing. Many see planning as being restrictive and prefer to allow the words to 'just flow'.

That's fine, but as we've already discussed, the majority of today's novel writing is a potentially commercial enterprise and most typescripts we see at these workshops are a long way from being the finished product the authors believe them to be. Successful novel writing requires a lot more discipline if we're going to get it right this time.

Exercise: Session 2 – Theme, Plot and Structure

1. Describe the nature of the theme of your novel.
2. Drawing on the 150 word 'blurb' from the last session, suggest a couple of ideas that might provide a convincing sub-plot; or describe an existing sub-plot.

3. What period and time span will the novel cover … and why? Think about it.

4. Taking this session into account, have you any further observations on where your novel might become bogged down. Can you see any potential problems?

5. Prepare a structure breakdown for the first five chapters, showing where you intend to introduce the characters and 'action'.

and check out The Horror Fiction Review

This blog offers reviews for fans of horror fiction by fans of horror fiction. "We rarely print super-negative reviews unless we feel a book truly deserves it (our biggest criticism is that we like everything we read. This is the furthest thing from the truth – many books we read do not make it into this e-zine) … This is a fanzine. If you want more critical reviews, a fanzine might not be the best place to look."

http://thehorrorfictionreview.blogspot.ie/

Chapter Four

Fakelore and Fantasy
(Dennis Wheatley, *et al.*)

In the deep, dank recesses of the imagination there is always the vision of a vaulted subterranean chamber. The impenetrable stone walls suppurating moisture like globules of blood, glisten in the candle light, as flickering cowled shadows perform a sinister dance macabre by the high altar. The fetid air mingles with the reek of incense as the high priest prepares to conduct the most blasphemous of all satanic rites of the witches' sabbat – the Black Mass.

This is the opening paragraph to my latest novel, *The House of Strange Gods*, which can hardly be said to lack that essential impact – although there *is* a twist in this particular tale. In attempting to portray the ultimate in depredation, however, past writers of Gothic horror have drawn heavily on these supposed satanic and sabbatical elements of the black mass and, as a result, have created a grotesque chimera that has robbed fact of its reason – which would no longer pass muster in contemporary horror fiction, unless there is a historical slant.

Based on the genuine French Court scandal of the seventeenth century, the Chambre Ardente Affaire brought rumour of the black mass to public attention for the first time, painting lurid pictures of frenzied priests sprinkling the breasts of a naked girl with blood from a newborn baby. The Affaire had all the trappings of a best selling horror novel but it is generally believed that it wasn't until the nineteenth century that a 'few wayward minds' created the black mass as it is thought of today. Some even trace this claim back to the eighteenth-century literary invention of the Marquis de Sade's most infamous fiction, *Justin*, in which the heroine herself tells of the indignities she suffered during the rite.

It is probably this fictional account of de Sade's, coupled with the factual account of the Chambre Ardente Affaire, which has provided every occult-horror novelist with the standard format for a black mass. With this blueprint for debauchery and depravity, the Gothic horror genre was eagerly exploited by classic writers such as 'Monk' Lewis and J K Huysmans, whose novel *La-Bas* (*Down There*) caused a sensation when it first appeared in 1891 because of the 'extraordinarily detailed and vivid descriptions' of the rite. The publisher's blurb on a later reprint claimed: "These descriptions are also authentic, for Huysmans had first-hand knowledge of the satanic practices, witch-cults and the whole of the occult underworld then thriving in Paris."

Much of the same was claimed for the occult novels written by Dennis Wheatley, whose *The Devil Rides Out*, was hailed by James Hilton as "The best thing of its kind since *Dracula*". *The Fortean Times* maintained that if William Blake's verdict on Milton was "of the Devil's party without knowing it", then much the same could be said of Dennis Wheatley. "He virtually invented the popular image of Satanism in twentieth-century Britain, and he made it seem strangely seductive. If the appeal of Black Magic in popular culture was ultimately erotic, then it was largely due to Wheatley's writing ... Thanks to Wheatley, people 'knew' what Black Magic and Satanism – historically an almost non-existent phenomenon – were like. Professor Jean La Fontaine made an astute link to Wheatley-derived imagery in her debunking of the Satanic Ritual Abuse panic ..."

Despite this, Guy N Smith still used these outdated ideas to publish *Nightspawn* in 2010 with the following scenario:

Terror comes to a peaceful village. Residents cower behind closed doors and closed curtains after dark, afraid to go outside. Sylvia has become a witch and with her coven practices satanic rites up on the heath ... Meanwhile the women of the village form a vigilante group to rid themselves of a witch who has seduced their husbands into the black arts. Soon there will be another death ...

On a more positive note, Wheatley supervised a series of 45 paperback reprints for Sphere Publishing under the collective heading of 'The Dennis Wheatley Library of the Occult', selecting the titles (including several traditional 'horrors' such as *Dracula, Frankenstein, Down There, Faust* and *The Monk*) and writing short introductions for each book. How many of these 'classics' have you read?

Dracula - Bram Stoker*
The Werewolf of Paris - Guy Endore
Moonchild - Aleister Crowley*
Studies in Occultism - Helena Blavatsky
Carnacki the Ghost-Finder - William Hope Hodgson
The Sorcery Review - Elliott O'Donnell
Harry Price: The Biography of a Ghost-Hunter - Paul Tabori
The Witch of Prague - F Marion Crawford*
Uncanny Tales 1 - selected by Dennis Wheatley
The Prisoner in the Opal - AEW Mason
The Devil's Mistress - JW Brodie-Innes
You and Your Hand – Cheiro
Black Magic - Marjorie Bowen
Real Magic - Philip Bonewits
Faust – Goethe*
Uncanny Tales 2 - selected by Dennis Wheatley
The Gap in the Curtain - John Buchan
The Interpretation of Dreams – Zolar
Voodoo - Alfred Metraux
The Necromancers – R H Benson*

Satanism and Witches - essays & stories selected by Dennis Wheatley

The Winged Pharaoh - Joan Grant*

Down There – J K Huysmans*

The Monk - Matthew Lewis*

Horror at Fontenay - Alexandre Dumas

The Hell-Fire Club - Donald McCormick*

The Mighty Atom - Marie Corelli

The Affair of the Poisons - Frances Mossiker

The Witch and the Priest - Hilda Lewis

Death by Enchantment - Julian Franklyn

Fortune Telling by Cards - Ida Prangley

Dark Ways to Death - Peter Saxon

The Ghost Pirates - William Hope Hodgson

The Phantom of the Opera - Gaston Leroux

The Greater Trumps - Charles Williams

The Return of the Magi - Maurice Magre

Uncanny Tales 3 - selected by Dennis Wheatley

King Is a Witch - Evelyn Eaton*

Frankenstein - Mary Shelley*

Curse of the Wise Woman - Lord Dunsany

Brood of the Witch Queen - Sax Rohmer

Brazilian Magic: Is It the Answer? - Pedro McGregor

Darker than You Think - Jack Williamson

War in Heaven - Charles Williams

Morwyn - John Cowper Powys

I can count eleven – but titles that don't appear on the listing and possibly should have done are *The Exorcist* (1971) by William Peter Blatty, based on an allegedly genuine 1949 exorcism; *The Conjurers* (1974) by Marilyn Harris, described as 'a soul-freezing novel of an occult experiment and diabolical possession'; *The Wicker Man* (1979) by Robin Hardy and Antony Shaffer that needs no introduction – and the fiction of American author

Howard Phillips Lovecraft, which has given birth to a whole new cult, based on some "fifty-three stories and assorted fragments ... all of which are based upon a bizarre and terrifying occult mythology."

Originally written for the cheap pulp horror magazines of his time (1890-1917), they have subsequently gained a reputation for having genuinely powerful occult significance. According to *The Occult Source Book*, Lovecraft developed a "mythology centering on 'dread Cthulu' – concentrated evil and powers of darkness struggling through to control the world, knowledge of which is contained in a variety of evil books, especially the *Necronomicon* – an imaginary book created by Lovecraft, but one which, after his invention of it, was spoken of as really existing by some subsequent authors."

By contrast (and also unlisted by Wheatley) is Arthur Machen, regarded as one of the finest of Welsh mystical writers, who *was* for a short time, a member of the Order of the Golden Dawn, although most of his best stories have a "hint of pantheist mystery about them, and are far away from the theatre of ritual". His most spine-tingling works include *The Great God Pan* (1890), *The Hill of Dreams* (1895) and *The Three Imposters* (1895).

Another sub-genre concerns the ancient Egyptian un-dead that started with *The Mummy!: or A Tale of the Twenty-Second Century*, an 1827 novel written by Jane C. Loudon, about an Egyptian mummy brought back to life in the twenty-second century. There are lots of parallels with Mary Shelley's *Frankenstein* and the plot features one of the earliest known examples of a 'mummy's curse'. Europe was in the grip of 'Egyptomania' at the time and this was subsequently reflected in the literature of the day. Other principal novels in the genre malign two of the great heroes of ancient Egyptian history (*The Mummy, or Ramses the Damned* (1989) by Anne Rice) Rameses II (known as 'the Great') and Imhotep a court architect from the Pyramid Age. The latter, *The Mummy* (1999), is a novel by Max

Allan Collins based on the film of the same name – a "tale of living inhumation, reincarnation, warped passion and other multifarious horrors" that dates from around the 1930s. According to screenwriter Martin Pallot, these walking dead were generally given their semblance of life either by secret spells written on ancient papyrus, or by the need to fulfil a terrible curse.

The best of the bunch, not surprisingly, is Bram Stoker's *The Jewel of the Seven Stars*, a Victorian tale of reincarnation on a much more credible level – in that it is the dead Egyptian queen's own will that determines her fate. This is a true Gothic horror/romance with plenty of adventure and a steely female lead, and yet *The Jewel* is often absent from Stoker's crown:

> Their faces were black, and their hands and necks were smeared with blood which had burst from mouth and nose and eyes. On the throat of each were the marks, now black-ening, of a hand of seven fingers. Trelawny and I drew close, and clutched each other in awe and fear as we looked. For, most wonderful of all, across the breast of the mummied Queen lay a hand of seven fingers, ivory white, the wrist only showing a scar like a jagged red line, from which seemed to hang drops of blood.

It is easy to become confused by all the sub-sub-genres within horror writing that were created out of the necessity of having to label everything and file it into its correct category! Firstly we had 'urban Gothic' influenced by industrial and post-industrial urban society pioneered in the mid-nineteenth century in Britain and the United States with novels such as Robert Louis Stevenson's *Strange Case of Dr Jekyll and Mr Hyde* (1886); Oscar Wilde's *The Picture of Dorian Gray* (1890) and Bram Stoker's *Dracula* (1897). And if we turn to Wikipedia we discover even more developments:

From the twentieth-century urban Gothic helped to spawn other sub-genres, including Southern Gothic, using the Southern United States as a location, and later Suburban Gothic, which shifted the focus from the urban centre to the residential periphery of modern society. Since the 1980s Gothic horror fiction and urban Gothic in particular has revived as a genre, with series of novels like Anne Rice's *Vampire Chronicles* and Poppy Z. Brite's *Lost Souls*, both making New Orleans a key centre of Gothic fantasy. Urban Gothic themes and images were also used in comics and graphic novels, including Frank Miller's *Daredevil* (1979), *Batman* (1986) and *Sin City* series (1991), James O'Barr's *The Crow*, beside Alan Moore's *From Hell* (1991) and *The League of Extraordinary Gentlemen* (1999).

The fact that horror is generally pure fantasy should not lessen the enjoyment of either the writer or the reader for these historical fabrications, for human curiosity has always been drawn towards the arcane. Rather let the reader marvel at the realms of depravation and grotesqueness that the darker side of fantasy can produce, for in the dark, dank recesses of the imagination there will always be a vision of a vaulted subterranean chamber ... producing the **terror of an extreme rational fear of some accepted form of reality and the dread of the use of systematic violence.**

Ideas and Inspiration

The only way to utilise these aspects of fantasy-horror is to cast the story in an historical setting, in order to draw upon the more gruesome and fictitious elements. From the writer's perspective this enables us to exploit the mistakes made by earlier authors but we need to understand which of these 'potboilers' give us the best examples of the fakelore and fantasy sub-genre. One of the best in literary style must be *The Conjurers* by Marilyn Harris, which has some truly spine-chilling moments, and in terms of commercial horror we'd have to go a long way to beat the necrophiliac sex and violence of Richard Matheson's *Hell House* in leaving a lasting impression! *The Vampires of Alfama* exist in some sort of parallel universe and the author draws upon all the gruesome effects of Inquisitional sadism. And although not half as bad as they were painted, *The Hell-Fire Club* by Donald McCormick suggests that there could be a lot of Regency mileage for an enterprising writer to draw upon.

Session 3 – Characterisation

Whether your horror novel is plot-led, or character-led it will not generate any appeal unless the reader can empathise with the main characters. They can love or hate your 'lead' but they do need to feel *something*. As a starting point, let's consider the following:

- If you don't care about your characters, neither will the reader react when they are 'killed off'.

- Characters must be credible, but they don't have to be likeable!

- Avoid stereotypical characters and cardboard cut-outs who are there merely to provide canon fodder for the forces of evil.

- A strong supporting cast *is* essential for a well-balanced story.

In most cases, the novel starts with a germ of an idea relating to how a certain character is going to think about, react, or experiment with, the 'manifestation' that the plot throws at him/her. In a nutshell, this central character is the pivot around whom the rest of the story is constructed – and you the author will have to maintain the reader's sympathy/empathy/hatred for him/her for the next 80,000+ words. You'll know when you've got it right because the character will become real for *you*. You will be equally aware of their reaction in the same way that you know your closest friend would, or would not, react to something that went against their principles. **Your character must be real to you or they will not be real for the reader**. The reader must want your character to win through, whatever the odds. And in horror fiction these odds can often appear insurmountable!

Which brings us to the credibility of your characters within the story. Unless we're talking about fantasy, supermen or women really don't work, simply because there is no provision for failure, or the human elements that provide conflict and misunderstanding – particularly in horror fiction.

The main characters must also fit comfortably within the period or setting of the story. When we are talking about credibility, we are also talking about character flaws that can make the man or woman more appealing or sympathetic.

One of our authors created a character who, in her youth, was too intense and self-obsessed and had we worked through the occult novel from A to B there would have been very little about the girl to make us care whether she lived or died. In this case, the author told the story in flashbacks from the vantage point of an eighty-year old woman, who could see all too clearly with the benefit of hindsight, just how much her intense and selfish behaviour had cost her dear. We like and respect the older woman for her honesty, and therefore are more sympathetic towards her younger self as the story unfolds.

Think back to the sadistic camp guard in *Merry Christmas Mr Lawrence*, whose geniality belied his callous treatment of the POWs. Then there was the film director who told a scriptwriter that he could totally destroy his image of a hardened contract killer, by having the man stop and stroke a cat, while on his way to a kill. These subtle nuances can add depth to what could be perceived as a one-dimensional character. It's also very easy for the subconscious to take over the 'drawing' of characters. As one author found to her horror, when she discovered that in her draft typescript, all her 'goodies' were blonde, and all her 'baddies' were dark haired! Was this a subconscious throw-back to the days of black and white films, when the good guys wore white hats and the bad guys wore black? This is what we mean by stereotyping – when characters are *so* predictable that their appearance and behaviour become almost a cliché.

Another typescript that came our way featured the heroine (a gentle and rather colourless creature) and her rival, a glamorous ball-breaker. The problem with the story was that the author had made the 'vamp' so consistently awful that it was impossible to see why the chap they were fighting over, was attracted to her in the first place. To break the impasse it was suggested that there should be a few added dimensions to the glamour-girl person- ality to at least make her credible and give reasons for her behaviour. The author's reaction was that she *wasn't supposed to be liked and that there wasn't any good to be found in her anyway*. The real reason, one suspects, is that the 'heroine' was so wet, that any quarter given her protagonist would have merely made her appear even wetter!

Unfortunately, in many of the early Gothic horror novels, the Victorian 'shrinking violet' is often a source of exasperation to the modern reader – which may also explain why Bram Stoker's *Dracula* has proved so popular with female readers. Mina Harker is a gentle soul but in the face of adversity, she has the strength of a Toledo blade that gains her the respect of her male companions.

Ironically, it's the 'manly virtues' of these males with their virile Victorian posing and posturing, which would encourage any modern red-bloodied female to decide to run off with her vampire lover!

Characters that move woodenly through the story *will* bog down the action and bore the reader to death, long before your 'evil being' has got around to finishing them off. In *How to Plot Your Novel,* Jean Saunders reflects that allowing characters to grow as the plot develops may work for experienced authors but that it "can be a disastrous assumption for a beginner to make". She maintains that creating a character profile for the central characters is as necessary as any other form of plotting. So spend some time producing a full CV for each of the important people involved in the story and indicate where their lives interact with the others. Just remember that no character should be 100 per cent perfect.

Although they are not often an integral part of the plot, minor characters are equally as important and can provide:

- light relief
- help in moving the story along
- chance encounters
- red herrings
- wisdom
- the throwing of a spanner in the works

Minor characters should be there to serve a purpose and for that we should turn to the greatest 'bit player' writer of them all: Shakespeare. He created bit parts throughout his plays that are often the ones audiences remember – like the gatekeeper in *Macbeth,* for instance – the only 'bit' of light relief in the whole play. Minor characters can be the postmistress or housekeeper, and the focus of all village gossip – just think how many red herrings that one could provide and she only needs to appear as a 'bit player' throughout.

Beware, however, of creating a supporting player who appears quite frequently at the beginning and then sinks without trace, and for no apparent reason – this is more common than you would believe. Minor characters are there to move the plot and dialogue along when the author feels it is necessary to inject a piece of information, but doesn't want it imparted by the main characters. Here are two simple tricks for creating the perfect blend of 'people' for your novel:

1. The casting couch. How many times have you been disappointed by the casting when a favourite book has been turned into a film or television series? Use this process in reverse and think of an actor who has played a similar part to the one required in your novel. Mentally take the image and superimpose it onto the character you wish to create. In other words, if you were casting your own novel as a film, who would you get to play the parts – both main and supporting roles?

2. Astrology. There are plenty of books around on the subject (try the charity shops) that give the positive and negative traits of all the 'sun signs' and I know several authors who use this method to create multi-dimensional characters by using a fictitious birth sign as a starting point. It will even help you sort out who is compatible, and who is a potential protagonist.

Choosing the right name for characters is also important because a name can say an awful lot about a person, without the need to go into a long and involved description. Avoid having two people whose names begin with the same letter (unless it's a comedy), i.e. Jason and Jayne, Robert and Rebecca, or James and Jamie. And watch those names, first and surnames, ending with 's'. Or you'll be forever writing James's; ... Mrs Prentiss's. Get the point? Names should reflect the fashion, society and history of the period, and avoid using something that no one can comfortably pronounce. One book that should be on every fiction writer's shelf is *The Oxford Names Companion*, which will provide endless sources for both first and surnames, as well as place-names.

A character's occupation should also be an integral part of the story. There's no point in slinging in the fact that Cyril is a retired antiques dealer and not exploiting this to the full in the narrative – especially if you need a 'cursed artifact' to get things moving. Your story will revolve around the main character's occupation, so more than a little detail needs to appear, if only to convince the reader that they are about to enter this particular world. Unless your plot centres on the double-dealing of high finance, then an art expert, fighter pilot, or racehorse trainer is going to appear much more glamorous than a commodities broker – but would any of these be of use in a horror plot? And how come I've so much information about horror films and novels to hand? One of my characters in *House of Strange Gods* happens to be a horror buff and this was part of my research.

One of the best examples of creating a character in the reader's mind is the style of interview found every weekend in the colour supplements. Bearing in mind that lengthy description is 'out', obtain a few back issues and study the way that the interview is constructed. The angle is usually related to the celeb's current work but throughout the 3,000-word piece, there will be single sentences that skillfully describe what the subject is wearing, appearance, mannerisms, attitude, etc. This is the approach you should aim for when developing your character's personality throughout the narrative. Sharp, incisive thumb-nail sketches rather than lengthy description allow the reader to recreate the 'person' in their mind's eye and participate in the story, rather than just being a casual observer. This device is particularly useful when writing horror fiction where action is paramount.

Publisher Krystina Kellingley offers this bit of advice:

Just as we all have to juggle things we have to do in our

everyday life, the author must also include different things into the plot for his characters to do. That multi-tasking is what makes them real. The author also needs to multi-task by layering the story. Essentially the bones of any horror story are the eternal struggle between good and evil. The author's task is to set this against a new backdrop. Not only must our hero/heroine fight evil, they must also deal with their inner demons, try to protect people they love, stop the innocent being hurt, possibly earn a living, and probably get emotionally involved with someone they come across whilst on their mission.

If you've read any of my other blogs, you'll no doubt be aware that I place characterisation very high on the list of what makes a good novel of any genre. However, the horror genre is conspicuous by the need to get the reader's attention quickly. Not only does the author have to have a plot that is well-paced and sharp dialogue, he must have characters who are compelling from the start.

Exercise: Session 3 – Characterisation

1. In 150 words give the opposite characteristics of your main characters, i.e. what are the 'flaws' in your 'lead'; and what are the good points about the protagonist?
2. What is it about your main character that you like (a) best, and (b) least? What else could you add to make them more believable?
3. Have you paid enough attention to the occupation of your characters, or is it merely a throw-away piece of information? How can you exploit this in the plot?
4. Conduct an imaginary interview with your main character, using the style of the colour supplements. In 200 words, create a thumb-nail sketch of how they look, what they are wearing, manner, etc.;

43

5. Create a character profile for a secondary character, who will play an important, but minor role in your story.

and check out Trash Fiction/Horror

The books are grouped in various loose categories, with some titles appearing on more than one listing. There's also an A-Z index of both book titles and authors, and occasionally the site has books for sale. Virtually all pictures are links and each book is listed with publishing details, the blurb from the back of the cover and the site administrator's own comments on it. Includes full details of The Dennis Wheatley Library of the Occult under 'Wheatley'.

http://www.trashfiction.co.uk

Chapter Five

Chimera (Cross genre)

Mary Shelley's novel, *Frankenstein*, though clearly influenced by the Gothic tradition, is often considered the first science fiction novel, despite the omission in the narrative of any scientific explanation of the monster's animation and the focus instead on the moral issues and consequences of such a creation. There is also within the horror genre what is known as cross-genre or slip-stream – where two distinct themes are *deliberately* inter-woven – such as science fictional horror, historical fantasy, etc. One of the earliest writers to embrace the technique was H P Lovecraft (1890-1937), who created a unique blend of science fiction and supernatural horror. In 'H P Lovecraft: The Case for the Defence', Ian Morland explains:

For the enthusiastic reader, it is fascinating to see how seminal ideas emerged and were developed by Lovecraft, and how different currents of thought came to overlap and mingle during his career. Locations vary enormously across geography and history to accommodate these developments. Lovecraft's semi-historical world of turn-of-the-century New England, his own favourite narrative background, merges with pure fantasy of supernatural and primeval forces. Yet other tales are woven entirely in alien worlds which strangely parallel ours. Most famously, many of Lovecraft's tales refer to a sinister race of beings which live in other dimensions, after losing their places in this world by abusing the dark forces.

Lovecraft's world was originally created for the pulp-fiction market but has subsequently acquired a reputation for the author as a cult-figure. According to the entry in *The Occult Source Book*: "He developed a mythology centering on the 'dread Cthulu', concentrated evil and powers of darkness struggling to break through and control the world, knowledge of which is contained in a variety of evil books, especially the 'Necronomicon' – an imaginary book created by Lovecraft, but one which, after his invention of it, was spoken of as really existing by some subsequent authors."

One contemporary horror author with links to Lovecraft and worthy of study is Brian Lumley, who expanded on the Cthulu-cult stories and later wrote the 'Necroscope' series of novels, including the *Vampire World Trilogy* (*Blood Brothers*, *The Last Aerie* and *Bloodwars*). Lumley has since become recognised as an international 'horror phenomenon' with books published in 13 countries, with more than 2 million books sold in the Necroscope series alone. His own brand of writing is a fine example of the dividing lines between the slip-stream of fantasy and horror, or science fiction and horror.

Mary Shelley's *Frankenstein* appeared "as society anxiously awaited the dramatic changes that the industrial revolution would bring. Her Gothic fantasy captures perfectly our fears today about what science and technology hold in store. Genetic engineering may soon allow scientists to create human beings to orders ..." observed Jennie Grey, critic for *Udolpho* magazine, in response to the release of Kenneth Branagh's film version of *Frankenstein*.

Subsequent cross genre novels also reflected fears about what science and technology hold in store and the re-occurring theme of world domination by an alien species. Possibly the first in the modern sub-genre of horror/science fiction was *The Day of the Triffids* (1951) by John Wyndham, a post-apocalyptic novel about a plague of blindness which befalls the entire world, which allows for the rise of an aggressive species of plants. It has since been made into a feature film (1962); three radio drama series

(1957, 1968 and 2008), and two TV series (1981 and 2009); in 2003 the novel was listed on the BBC's survey 'The Big Read'.

Although not strictly a novel, Quatermass was a fictional scientist, originally created by the writer Nigel Kneale for BBC television; intelligent and highly moral, Professor Quatermass continually finds himself confronting these sinister alien forces that threaten to destroy humanity. The character also appeared in films, on the radio and in print over a fifty-year period from the 1950s. Because of the series' popularity, a script book for *The Quatermass Experiment*, including some photographs from the production, was released by Penguin Books in 1959; followed by similar releases of *Quatermass II* and *Quatermass and the Pit*, both published in 1960. Arrow Books also released a 'novelisation' of the 1979 *Quatermass* serial, written by Kneale, which was written during production, and contained many additional scenes and extra background detail not included in the original scripts.

The Space Vampires (1976) by Colin Wilson is a science fiction-horror novel, it is about the remnants of a race of intergalactic vampires who are brought back from outer space and let loose on Earth. These aliens are energy vampires, as opposed to the familiar blood-sucking variety, that consume the 'life force' by seducing living beings with a deadly kiss, and also have the ability to take control of their victims' bodies. Though initially the aliens' form appears to be a bat-like creature, the creatures are ultimately revealed to be beings from a higher dimension.

When it comes to contemporary cross-genre horror, suspense, science fiction and fantasy writers, the acknowledged king of the technique is undoubtedly Stephen King – starting with *Carrie* in 1974 he has sold more than 350 million books, many of the novels having been made into feature films. One of the most frequently banned books in American schools, the novel revolves around a shy high-school girl, who uses her newly discovered telekinetic powers to exact revenge on those who tease her; while *Salem's*

Lot (1975) concerns an isolated town that is infested with vampires.

Pet Sematary is a (1983) horror novel about a pet cemetery – where the children of the town bury their deceased animals, most of them dogs and cats killed by the trucks on the road – and adjoining an ancient burial ground that was once used by the Micmacs, a Native American tribe. A boy buries his cat there but the next afternoon, the cat returns home, although acting strangely and with an unpleasant odour – revealing that the burial ground has restorative powers. *It* (1986) follows the exploits of seven children as they are terrorised by an eponymous being, which exploits the fears and phobias of its victims in order to disguise itself while hunting its prey. 'It' primarily appears in the form of a clown in order to attract its preferred prey of young children. While *The Tommyknockers* (1987), although in the horror genre, is more of an excursion into the realm of science fiction as the residents of a Maine town gradually fall under the influence of a mysterious object buried in the woods.

This is vintage Stephen King horror, taken from the 50-plus titles and short story collections published by him over the years, and we can do no more than quote his own formula for learning to write well, and as a guide to producing his quota of 2000 words per day. "Read and write four to six hours a day. If you cannot find the time for that, you can't expect to become a good writer." His excursion into how-to techniques is covered by *On Writing: A Memoir of the Craft* (2000) also contains valuable advice for would-be novelists.

James Herbert also has the imagination to incorporate other genres into his horror writing, including killer rats (*Rats* 1974); scientific disaster (*The Fog* 1975); ghost stories; several thrillers with elements of the supernatural; neo-Nazism (*The Spear* 1978); reincarnation (*Fluke* 1977 and *Nobody True* 2003); a haunted house (*The Secret of Crickley Hall* 2006) and an alternative history of

WWII. He released a new novel virtually every year from 1974 to 1988, wrote six novels during the 1990s and has released three in the 2000s. "I am very insecure about being a writer", he stated in the book *Faces of Fear*, "I don't understand why I am so successful. And the longer I stay that way, the better it's going to be, because that's what keeps me on the edge, striving if you like."

Dean Koontz is best known for his suspense thrillers, but also frequently incorporates elements of horror, science fiction, mystery and satire into his novels. He began writing suspense and horror fiction in the 1970s, both under his own name and several pseudonyms, sometimes publishing up to eight books a year. According to the entry in Wikipedia: "Many of Koontz's pseudonymous novels are now available under his real name. Many others remain suppressed by Koontz, who bought back the rights to ensure they could not be republished; he has, on occasion, said that he might revise some for re-publication, but only three have appeared – *Demon Seed* and *Invasion* were both heavily rewritten before they were republished ..."

Cross-genre horror novels more often than not reflect a science-based scenario because of its potential to create 'monsters', although there are also endless possibilities of using historical backgrounds to re-activate monstrous energies from the past – especially those with a bloody history – such as Aztec, the Inquisition, Nazi Germany, Mau-Mau, etc. Both approaches will, of course, require a tremendous amount of research to make the horror convincing but history has a wealth of detail to draw on to recreate authentic scenarios. Horror can also manifest in crime writing if the story is gory enough to produce **the terror of the use of systematic violence.**

Ideas and Inspiration

For the horror novelist with the ability to create 'other worlds', the universe of science and fantasy is wide open for them;

although there are still certain rules to be observed – ie. the laws of physics and magic – the creative options for the writer are infinite. The key is being able to think in the future, just as Leonardo de Vinci, Jules Verne and H G Wells were able to do – and then put your own horror spin onto the futuristic concept of having two worlds colliding. With the gigantic leaps forward in science, genetic engineering and quantum physics there is very little that we should consider to be beyond the realms of credibility when it comes to encountering other worlds, or bringing something through to this world – for example Colin Wilson's *Space Vampires* and *Stargate, which* is described as military science fiction. A series of five novels written by Bill McCay were published from 1996 to 1999, based on the story of the 1994 film, *Stargate*, based on a ring-shaped alien 'gateway' that created a wormhole enabling personal teleportation to similar devices located cosmic distances away. Although gratuitous horror is absent from *Stargate*, there is no reason why a similar concept should not catapult the reader into a *Concrete Jungle* (1995: by Nathan Archer from the *Predator* series) scenario. Disaster themes can also fall into the horror genre – whether natural or man-made – because of the sheer scale of the devastation involved and the horrific ways there are for people to die!

Session 4: Pace and Narrative Style

The pace and narrative style of any novel is all about holding the reader's attention and making them want to turn the page. In *Writing a Novel*, Nigel Watts tells us that the reader's attention will be held mostly by the author raising intriguing questions and delaying the answer. "Although a single important question may be enough motivation for a novel, significant questions should be raised in every chapter." These 'questions' should be automatically raised as part of the natural flow of the horror story and the viewpoint of the narrative/narrator.

It doesn't matter how good your idea for a plot, or how charismatic your main characters, if the pace and narrative style doesn't hold the interest and sympathy of the publisher's reader, then the submission will fail.

Pace

All novels have a time frame. From 'A Day in the Life of ... ' to a grand epic like *War and Peace*, that charts a family saga over a number of years. In *How to Plot Your Novel*, Jean Saunders suggests that this should be one of the first things you think about when plotting a novel because this can be one of the easiest ways for a beginner to start. "Once you do this, you have parameters to work within. Your characters must achieve their goals and aspirations within certain time limits. And you can plan and pace your plot accordingly."

To echo the point raised by Krystina Kellingley in the previous chapter, many first-time novelists will begin their story much too far in advance of the actual 'plot', which means that the opening impact is delayed because we are wasting time scene-setting and working up to the real beginning of the novel. If we are writing a horror novel, then we need to cut to the chase to hook the reader's interest.

So ... whether you set your story over fifty years, five years, five months, five days or five hours the pace is of paramount importance. If the pace is too fast or too slow, then you will not hook the publisher's reader either. In truth, the passage of time within the story is often a major problem for new horror writers because they find it difficult to balance the time frame for the beginning, the middle and the end of the action. Some parts become barren wastelands because there is no purposeful action; in other parts the action is crammed into single gory episodes because nothing of interest has been introduced to enhance the plot.

This is where we need to learn the subtle techniques of

moving the plot along. Of course, our characters need to have backgrounds, histories and pasts to make them credible but we don't need to clutter up the proceedings in order to reveal these in chapter and verse, especially where this sort of detail slows a horror novel down.

Firstly, look with a critical eye and decide if your current plot is really adequate for the length of time in which the story is set in terms of action. Novels, like life, are made up of peaks and troughs but it would not be advisable to include every trivial detail just to fill the pages. By using a 'plotting graph', try to contain the story within a realistic time frame with very little slack water in between. Your graph should show the high points of action (with brief notes), with the lows giving the opportunity for character development and 'padding'. Even in horror fiction there should still be peaks and troughs of action and inaction. The graph enables you to plan when certain dramatic interludes can be introduced into which chapters, and where the reader needs a respite from a surfeit of 'orrible 'appenings. Plot each chapter with as much attention to detail as the whole novel. Using this technique enables you to decide *exactly* when you are going to suspend the action in order to keep the reader in suspense and encourage them to read on.

The action is the easy part, simply because this is what drives the story along and it is probably already mapped out in your head. What we need to concentrate on now is how to introduce the more intimate and/or personal details that will flesh out our characters, *without holding up the action.* The following are simple devices but they are extremely effective for adding depth to the character without resorting to lengthy description and/or narrative.

Flashbacks
A device for giving readers information about a person, place or event that happened before the novel began. Here a character can

have a past memory triggered by a happening in the here and now, which helps the reader to understand his or her actions or responses to a current situation. Flashbacks enable us to filter information in a subtle way that does not hold up the action and gives the reader information on a need to know basis, which can only add to the suspense – but don't overdo the sauce and use them sparingly.

Dialogue

Dialogue should *always* move the story along and if it doesn't, then it is superfluous. Again, if you need to inform the reader of something that happened before the start of the story, then it can be introduced in the form of a conversation between two or more people. Think in terms of 'real' dialogue and how much information you would give away to a stranger. "Tell me about yourself" isn't an invitation to start at pre-school and work your way through to retirement.

Reverie

The use of a character's thought processes allows us to convey the type of intimate or personal details that the character may not want to reveal openly. Often presented in italics, reverie can be used to express the character's real thoughts, while the dialogue is saying something completely different. Reverie can also be utilised if the character is alone and running over events in their mind prior to action. It is a method of recalling events that may have been subtly introduced earlier in the story.

Written Word

A clever way of dispensing with pages of unnecessary scene-setting is the employment of a letter, newspaper clipping or diary that can speak volumes about why events have come to pass: this technique was used extremely effectively by Bram

Stoker for *Dracula*.

Narrative style

Narrative style or viewpoint is the method we choose to tell the story. Many beginner novelists start off by writing in the first person but often find they run out of steam, simply because everything that happens must be seen, heard and experienced by the character telling the story. Working with 'I' very quickly becomes tedious, since 'I' cannot be everywhere at once and commenting on everyone and everything – especially in a horror novel. Having said that, Nigel Watts had this to say: "Because the readers can know only what the protagonist knows, it is easy for the author to spring surprises on them. Suspense and tension, therefore, often work well with a first person viewpoint."

Third person narrative is much easier to attempt and, depending on the length and/or structure of the story, we can chose either the third person single viewpoint or the third person multiple viewpoint. The third person single viewpoint can be equally as restrictive as first person narrative. This is less personal but your principal character needs to be strong enough to carry the whole novel on his or her shoulders. As Nigel Watts observes: "In order to make the character credible and authoritative, you will need to be privy to his or her thoughts, seeing the world through your character's eyes. Although it is important to know all your main characters well, you should know your 'viewpoint character' inside out."

If using the multi-viewpoint, it is advisable to stick to one at a time, because the reader will quickly become bored if they are constantly trying to work out who is doing or saying what, and to whom. Decide which of your characters will play out a particular scene – and stick to it: the easiest way to deal with multi-viewpoint is to utilise it chapter by chapter but do limit the number of character-viewpoints to the main players.

Tense

Novels are normally set in the past or present tense, and alternating tenses can also be confusing unless some clear demarcation line is drawn. In a recent submission the author used the present tense to convey the elderly characters' thoughts and reflection, and the past tense to tell the story.

The tense you choose is all part of the narrative style and if you find that the story isn't working in, say, the present tense, change it over to past tense and see if it flows more easily.

Exercise – Session 4: Pace and Narrative Style

1. Note your reasons for setting the novel within the chosen time frame and plot your graph showing the peaks and troughs of dramatic action throughout the chapter breakdown.

2. Calculate a rough estimate of how many chapters you think your novel will take, and be honest about whether your plot is adequate for its length.

3. Are there any areas where you feel your novel is showing signs of weakness. Make a note of these for future reference.

4. How many viewpoints do you intend to use throughout the story? How many 'main' characters will be involved? How well do you know your principal character?

5. Is your story to be set in the past or present tense? Would any purpose be served for using both for added emphasis?

6. Do you intend to include any form of humour in the narrative? Are you using it for the sake of being funny, or is it intended to be a natural part of the narrative? Humour should be inserted carefully into horror fiction, although black humour can help to relieve tension.

and check out TTA Press: Black Static magazine

"The publisher is named after the magazine it founded in 1994,

The Third Alternative, which was renowned for its slipstream/horror fiction. With the arrival of *Interzone* it was no longer necessary to publish anything remotely SF or Fantasy in *The Third Alternative*, so we took the opportunity to focus on the magazine's darker side and give it a new title to emphasise the slight shift in focus ... *Black Static* has continued the TTA tradition of publishing horror fiction that pushes the genre envelope ..." TTA are always open to submissions of new horror and dark fantasy short stories of up to about 10,000 words in length. Just follow the simple guidelines detailed on the website and note that *all* submissions must be in hard copy only.

http://ttapress.com/blackstatic/guidelines/

Chapter Six

The Twilight World (Mind games)

When it comes to horror novels of the mind (excluding the crime and detection genre) the greatest of all must surely be *Psycho* (1959) by Robert Bloch, and loosely based on the crimes of Wisconsin murderer and grave robber, Ed Gein, who lived just 40 miles from the author. The screenplay for the Hitchcock film based on the novel, however, was written by Joseph Stefano, and it is this masterpiece that horror aficionados remember rather than the original novel, and 'Norman Bates' became a buzz-word for someone sinister and creepy! But this wasn't the first horror novel to achieve such distinction.

Similarly, the phrase 'Jekyll and Hyde' also became part of the language following the publication of Robert Louis Stevenson's *Strange Case of Dr Jekyll and Mr Hyde* in 1886. In this novella, Dr Jekyll assumes two completely different personalities, one good and kind and the other – Mr Hyde – violent and totally immoral. This 'split personality' was due to the drinking of a 'potion' as part of an experiment, but the evil personality gained the upper hand. Similarly, 'Jack the Ripper' type novels which fall into the 'splatter' sub-genre due to the graphic details of mutilation, can also be credited to the horror writer's pen.

An even earlier example, are the writings of Edgar Allan Poe, which focussed "less on the traditional elements of Gothic literature and more on the psychology of his characters as they often descended into madness." [*The Complete Tales and Poems of Edgar Allan Poe*] His most famous stories, *The Fall of the House of Usher* (1839), *Premature Burial* (1844), *The Pit and the Pendulum* (1842) are often more well-known as late-night horror movies and the demented antics of Vincent Price during the 1960s than for any regard for Poe's literary style.

The fear of interment, or being buried alive is probably one of the oldest terrors, but the European obsession with premature burial reached almost hysterical proportions in the late nineteenth century. It was not unknown for people to write clauses in their wills requesting posthumous decapitation, or at the very least the severing of the arteries of the neck and windpipe in order to 'make any revival in the grave absolutely impossible'. And while Poe was responsible for creating the classic work of fiction in his short story, *The Premature Burial*, there were many factual books and pamphlets available at the time.

This is a nightmare where fact is indeed more horrible than fiction and concerned a lawyer and member of Congress from Baltimore, whose wife 'died' and was entombed. But when the doors were reopened by the husband, some three years later, his wife's skeleton fell into his arms. The evidence showed that she had revived inside her coffin and her subsequent struggles had dislodged it from the ledge on which it rested causing it to break open on the floor. She had then endeavoured to attract help by beating on the iron doors of the vault with the remains of her own coffin and had finally collapsed through exhaustion. In falling, however, her shroud became entangled in some projecting ironwork, 'thus she remained and thus she rotted' ... erect'. [*The Unquiet Grave*, Martin Pallot]

The twilight world of the mind was the setting for Stephen King's *Misery* (1987), a psychological chiller of fan-fixation, when an author's decision to kill off the character of his 'Misery series' in order to re-establish himself as a mainstream writer, result in his being held captive by a mad woman. As the story progresses, he discovers a scrapbook of newspaper clippings suggesting that she murdered her own father, a college roommate, and numerous patients in several states—thirty-nine people in all. The horror escalates when she cuts off her captive's foot with an axe, cauterising the wound with a blowtorch, and slicing off his thumb with an electric knife!

Author Clive Barker's distinctive style is characterised by "the notion of hidden fantastical worlds coexisting with our own, the role of sexuality in the supernatural and the construction of coherent, complex and detailed universes ... bringing in the deeper, richer concepts of reality, the nature of the mind and dreams, and the power of words and memories" according to his entry in Wikipedia. His writing is described as 'urban fantasy with horror elements' where a magical world lies woven within a rug (*Weaveworld* 1987); a decades-long feud (*The Great and Secret Show* 1989) or the troubled life of a wildlife photographer (*Sacrament* 1996).

Again, with the supernatural horror novels of Ramsey Campbell, there is the breaking down of the boundaries between dream and reality (*Incarnate* 1983); or an entity attempting to gain entry to this world via the mind of a writer (*Midnight Sun* 1990). S T Joshi, literary critic, novelist, and a leading figure in the study of Howard Phillips Lovecraft and other authors of weird and fantastic fiction wrote: "Future generations will regard him as the leading horror writer of our generation, every bit the equal of Lovecraft or Blackwood."

Peter Straub's horror fiction has received numerous literary prizes such as the Bram Stoker Award, World Fantasy Award, and International Horror Guild Award. He wrote his first supernatural novel, *Julia* (1979) about a supernatural presence emerging following a séance; followed by *If You Could See Me Now* (1977), a tale of obsession and a vengeful spirit; and *Ghost Story* (1979), which became a national bestseller and cemented the author's reputation. Several horror novels followed, with growing success, including *The Talisman* (1984) and *Black House* (2001), two fantasy-horror collaborations with Straub's long-time friend and fellow author Stephen King.

Prolific British writer Graham Masterton was editor of *Mayfair* and the British edition of *Penthouse* before turning his hand to 'visceral sex' and horror. His first novel *The Manitou* (1976) was adapted for the film of the same name in 1978. His work has attracted critical acclaim, including a Special Edgar Award by the Mystery Writers of America for *Charnel House* (1988), and a Silver Medal by the West Coast Review of Books for *Mirror* (2011).

With over 5 million books in print, it's obvious that Robert McCammon was one of the most influential names in the horror literature boom of the late 1970s-early 1990s, with three titles (*The Wolf's Hour, Stinger,* and *Swan Song*) on the New York Times bestselling list. Like Dean Koontz, however, McCammon also refused to let his early novels be re-published because, "while not disliking the books, he does not feel that they are up to the standards of his later works. He wrote that he feels he was allowed to learn how to write in public, and therefore has decided to officially retire his earlier works." However, *Baal* and *Bethany's Sin* have since been re-released by Subterranean Press as limited editions.

In true pulp-fiction style, Guy N Smith introduces a blend of sex, violence and gore – and his work is described in the *Penguin Encyclopaedia of Horror and the Supernatural* as "imbued with lively storytelling and the tacky brilliance of the horror and science fiction cinema of the 1950s." This splatter-technique of his 70+ horror novels appears in such clichéd titles as *The Graveyard Vultures* and *Cannibal Cult* (1984 from the Sabat series); or *The Walking Dead* (1984 from the Pit series). Whatever we may think of his literary style, his work has attained considerable popularity since *Werewolf by Moonlight* was published in 1974, and in 1996 he published *Writing Horror Fiction* for A & C Black. *Nightspawn* was published in 2010 but most of his back titles are now available as e-books.

Amongst these titles we find both **terror in the extreme rational fear of some accepted form of reality, and horror as extreme irrational fear of the utterly unnatural or the super-**

natural. Moreover, there is realistic horror – the unnatural or supernatural fright presented in the guise of the normal.

Session 5: Bones and Padding

Writing the first draft of a horror novel is the easy part. You've off-loaded all the ideas, introduced an interesting sub-plot, got all the characters going in the right direction. There have been a few unexpected developments but nothing you couldn't handle — *but it still doesn't work.* There's something missing. These flaws usually manifest in what is sometimes referred to as 'the padding'. This is the element of the novel that adds depth and dimension to the story. This does not mean that pages of descriptive narrative can cure the problem because the solution is much more subtle than that.

Firstly, look at the characters you've created. Are they **real** enough for the reader to empathise with their traumas and difficulties, their lives and loves? Have you put too much emphasis on A's background, so that it becomes a total cop-out for decent feeling? Why are you, the author, justifying B's reaction to C, when you are condemning D for a similar mistake? Is *their* story believable?

Which brings us to the plot. Have you explored everyone's motives? Nobody does anything without a reason, valid or not, so is there sufficient explanation for X's behaviour to Y? Or does it sound hollow and contrived?

Going back to the points covered in Session Three, do you *really* care what happens to your characters? Because if you don't, how can you expect the reader to feel anything other than indifference? It's the interaction between characters that moves the plot along and gets the reader believing in it: if it's not working then it's back to the drawing board, I'm afraid.

Long physical descriptions need careful pruning, especially those usually found padding out Chapter One, since detailed descriptions aren't really necessary in horror novels – it's the personality that counts. If your heroine's eyes, instead of being 'liquid pools of sapphire blue' were replaced with 'eyes that developed a slight squint whenever she was nervous or uncomfortable', you kill two paragraphs with one edit. For horror writing in particular, physical description should only be used to imply character (which is why those colour-supplement interviews are such useful study exercises), and add depth to your story-telling. Today's readers are more interested in what goes on in a person's head, rather than being told how beautiful the heroine is, so cut the 'shimmering, long blonde hair' routine and concentrate more on body language. Spend some time with Desmond Morris's books on human behaviour *(Gestures, The Naked Ape, The Human Zoo, Manwatching,* etc.) and broaden your scope for characterisation. For example: one of those taking part in this course added a tantalising glimpse into her heroine's character by revealing that her designer clothes and accessories were all expensive fakes. Nice touch because it said quite a lot about the character without saying anything at all!

If you feel your characters have enough padding on their bones to make them real and compelling, what about the location of the action? Again, pages of descriptive prose will not necessarily give the right atmosphere to draw the reader into the story. A 500 word waffle on the herbaceous border incorporating the pride of the Sutton's seed catalogue, can probably be reduced to the 'astringent, dew-sharpened scent of ...' Lists of flora and fauna do not a novel make.

Also to be avoided are the *Miller's Antiques Guide* or a Pickford's removal inventory when it comes to house contents. Again you cannot create atmosphere from a furnishings or arts catalogue; neither does estate agent's parlance pass for good scene setting. **Atmosphere** is the key word when it comes to location, rather than tedious detail – especially for horror novels. If you can't see your location, how can you expect your reader to? If you're having problems with your location, invest in a few colour picture books showing the kind of place you've imagined, and which often reveal the idiosyncrasies of the owners in the way their personal belongings are casually scattered about. Don't copy – implement your own ideas. For example: in my latest novel I wanted to get away from the cliché of the old crumbling country house and instead used the idea of a combination of styles similar to Frank Lloyd Wright's 'Falling Water' and 'The Storer House'. 1930s Art Deco architecture isn't usually associated with modern Gothic but – so far – it's working!

Unless you're totally familiar with your subject, make sure you have sufficient reference books to hand to fill in the gaps, or take yourself off for a weekend break to somewhere similar to what you have in mind. At one novel workshop, a writer had her story taking place at a large country house, but the biggest stumbling block was the fact that she was totally unaware of how *real* country families run their houses and therefore the narrative didn't ring true. The large country house was an integral part of the plot and so it was suggested that she change the background to a family-owned country hotel to prevent any social gaffes being made. These changes also allowed for a greater diversity when it came down to the background of the characters involved.

We've also discussed the importance of getting the details right about characters' job descriptions. These background details also provide an extra dimension and should provide useful side roads and blind alleys for the plot to weave along. No detail should be brought into the story unless it has some part to play in moving the story along. In one murder mystery, the heroine was attracted to a local natural-fence maker but the only reference to this was when she arrived as his workshop to find him making fences! There was no hint as to why this man should have chosen this profession, or that he loved the outdoors and local wildlife ... and he was the hero!

The padding *is* an important part of the novel but not when it is included in order to knock up the word count. Extraneous detail sometimes has to be cut ruthlessly, even if this goes against the grain of our natural preferences and susceptibilities. Far from inhibiting our fine literary style, however, we could find that cutting actually improves it. Here are a few suggestions for improving your novel:

- Dispense with anything unnecessary. This sounds obvious but what *is* necessary? Only that which sets the scene, promotes the action, and activates the characters. The rest is ornament—though this too can play a part.

- Avoid over-description. Understatement and/or suggestion is often more effective.

- Never repeat information, unless for deliberate effect.

- Tightening sentences by shortening, especially in passages of tension.

- Make the dialogue racy and natural, perhaps by omitting the occasional pronoun.

- Don't sustain description for too long. Once the mood, setting or character is established (as succinctly as possible) forget it. Keep moving.

- Avoid slack 'tell all' dialogue. Remember: dialogue has three essential functions:

1 To pin-point and develop the character,
2 Further the action,
3 Usefully explain something previously unknown.

- Once any of these have been utilised there is no need to go on using the device.

- Use cross-conflicts or mini conflicts along the way.

- Make full use of suspense-tension, temporary relief, then more tension.

- Intrigue the readers by fresh additions. Hint subtly at things to come but make them wait.

The next stage of your novel is to now sit down and write through to the end. Remember that all the examples given are hypothetical problems, but every first novel is subject to some (if not all) of them, and every author who has ever written a novel has made the same errors in the early stages of their career. So don't be afraid to admit yours. There is a tremendous satisfaction in completing a novel but as with every form of saleable writing, you need to be much, much more than just a good writer. The secret is being your own sternest critic!

Exercise – Session 5: Bones and Padding

1 Describe briefly what you feel to be the most significant flaw in your novel at this stage of writing? What do you need to do to put it right? Are these major flaws, or merely 'technical hitches' that can be rectified at a later date as the novel progresses?

2 Have you put enough time and effort into researching background material for your location. Give a brief outline, in no more than 300 words, of the principal setting for the story and state why you have chosen this particular location.

3   Write a reasonably accurate 'job description' for your principal character, including qualifications, etc., necessary for the job. In other words, make it real.

4   Do you feel that you have enough material, background and focus to carry on with the first draft of the novel? If you are unsure, describe what you see as the problem?

5   Roughly speaking, how long do you think it will take you to finish the novel? Have you set yourself a deadline? If so, have you taken your family, job, holidays, etc. into account?

6   Are you happy with the changes, alterations, or different focus to the plot from when you sent in your first assignment?

and check out **Top 10 Horror Fiction: 2011, by Brad Hooper**
Booklist Online Book Review: Top 10 **Horror Fiction**: 2011.Hooper, Brad (author). FEATURE. First published August, 2011 (Booklist).Adult Books – Fiction – Horror.
www.booklistonline.com/Top-10-Horror-Fiction.../

Chapter Seven

Nature's Own

Animals are a popular theme in horror writing – usually in the guise of some friendly family pet that is destined to become the clichéd first blood-splattered victim of the 'presence' in whatever form it may take. A bouncy dog or curious cat will soon become a mangled mess of fur so that the writer can perpetrate mutilation and carnage in a build-up to killing off the human characters. It is also accepted within the FBI's behavioural sciences unit that the warning signs of certain mental disorders are a history of cruelty to animals (known as zoosadism), and is one of the traits that regularly appears in its computer records of serial rapists and murderers.

When it comes to terror from the natural world, however, we need look no further than *Jaws* by Peter Benchley for **the extreme** *rational* **fear of some accepted form of reality**. The novel tells the story of a great white shark that preys upon a small resort town and was inspired by several authentic incidents such as the Jersey Shore shark attacks of 1916 that resulted in four deaths over 12 days and the exploits of real-life shark hunter Frank Mundus.

The actual story (and success) of *Jaws* reads like a novel in itself. Doubleday commissioned Benchley to write the novel, while film producers Zanuck and Brown read it prior to publication and bought the film rights. Needless to say, this helped to raise the profile and when Jaws was published in 1974 it was an immediate success, staying on the bestseller list for some 44 weeks. By the time the film adaptation was released in June 1975 the book had sold 5.5 million copies domestically in the US alone, and eventually reached 20 million copies worldwide. Directed by Steven Spielberg, omitted many of the original subplots and focused on the shark. According to Wikipedia: "*Jaws* became the highest grossing movie in history up to that point, and is regarded as a watershed film in motion picture history, the father of the summer blockbuster film. It was followed by four sequels."

The Book of the Month Club dubbed it an 'A' book, followed by the *Reader's Digest*, so the publication date was delayed to allow for a "carefully orchestrated release". *Jaws* was released first in hardcover in February 1974, then as a book clubs' selection, followed by a national campaign for the paperback edition. Bantam bought the paperback rights for $575,000, which as Benchley points out, was "then an enormous sum of money".

In a later article written for the *National Geographic* 'Great White Sharks' (April 2000), Peter Benchley revealed that he felt responsible for the negative aspect in people's attitudes towards sharks that he felt *Jaws* had created. As a committed ocean conservationist he wrote: "Considering the knowledge accumulated about sharks in the last 25 years, I couldn't possibly write *Jaws* today ... not in good conscience anyway. Back then, it was generally accepted that great whites were anthropophagus (they ate people) by choice. Now we know that almost every attack on a human is an accident: The shark mistakes the human for its normal prey."

James Herbert's *The Rats*, published in the same year, also probably exacerbated the reaction of people towards the creature. This was his first novel and included gory depictions of mutilation and killing, including the opening sequence where a vagrant is attacked by a pack of dog-sized rats and eaten alive. The author had apparently drawn his inspiration from watching Tod Browning's *Dracula*; specifically the scene where Renfield describes his nightmare involving hordes of rats and linking the film to childhood memories he had of rats in the London suburbs. The entry in Wikipedi is also interesting in that it cites the social comments of the critics.

The first paperback edition sold out after three weeks. *The Rats* received harsh criticism upon its publication. It was deemed to be far too graphic in its portrayals of death and mutilation and that the social commentary regarding the neglect of London's suburbs was too extremist. For some reviewers, the novel was not literature, and not a good example of good writing. However, many consider the novel to be social commentary influenced by Herbert's harsh upbringing in immediate post-war London. The underlying theme of the novel is the lack of care by government toward the underclass and a lack of reaction to tragedy until it is too late. Fellow author Peter James stated: "I think Jim reinvented the horror genre and brought it into the modern world. He set a benchmark with his writing that many writers subsequently have tried, without success, to emulate."

Regardless of its critical unpopularity, *The Rats* was a success and followed by three sequels; *Lair* deals with a second outbreak of the mutants, this time in the countryside around Epping Forest rather than in the London slums; *Domain*, a nuclear war allows the rats to become the dominant species in a devastated city; and *The City*, an adventure set in the post-nuclear future.

Guy N Smith's imagination gave us mutant killer crabs in a series beginning with *Night of the Crabs* (1976) through to *Killer Crabs: The Return* (2012). The six novels chronicled an invasion of giant, man-eating crabs located along various parts of the British coastline. Smith's first novel, however, was: *Werewolf by Moonlight* (1974) with the clichéd *Return of the Werewolf* (1976) and *The Son of the Werewolf* (1978) completing the series.

The literary werewolf has a long history dating back to the Middle Ages but it was given a new lease of life during the nineteenth century where it became the classic tale of a man being transformed into the creature at the time of the full moon. The twentieth century witnessed the growth of the popularity of werewolf literature, with *The Werewolf of Paris* (1933) by Guy Endore being given classic status as the epitome of the werewolf sub-genre. In recent years the werewolf has taken a more heroic turn, as portrayed by Whitley Strieber in *The Wolfen* (1978) and *The Wild* (1991); while J K Rowling's Harry Potter series also reveals a more sympathetic portrayal. *The Company of Wolves* by Angela Carter (1979) gives another contemporary twist to the tale.

Guy N Smith has also written several horror novels with a growing body count and involving killer animals, including *Alligators* (1987) – not to be confused with the 1980 American horror film *Alligator*, where a giant reptile stalks the Chicago sewers.

Four Animal Rights activists break into their local zoo and free all the alligators in the Reptile House. This turns out to be a bad idea as two are soon eaten alive by killer Amazonian caimans, which then make a speedy exit into the nearby countryside. One of the group confesses everything to the local vet, who has been roped in to the 'gator hunt as the nearest thing to an expert on the creatures …

Cujo (1981) is a psychological horror novel by Stephen King, that won the British Fantasy Award in 1982, and was made into a film in 1983. In this story, a good-natured St Bernard is bitten by a rabid bat and turns into a mass killer before it is despatched in true horror style. Similar in style is *The Birds* (1952) by Daphne du Maurier (later made into a film by Alfred Hitchcock), where a community comes under attack by flocks of seabirds, which eventually becomes a national emergency.

There are, of course, certain animals on this planet that *are* fearsome in their own right, without the need for the horror writer's flight of fancy. Wolves, lions, leopards and bears have become man-eaters when age or injury prevents them from stalking their natural prey. Spiders from the 'primitive' mygalo-morphae family – which includes tarantulas and the Australian funnel-web – are heavy bodied and stout-legged, and take their name from the 'orientation of the fangs which point straight down'. Venomous snakes with the highest human mortality rate are the black mamba, coastal taipan, common krait and the king cobra. While in the water we find sharks and crocodiles waiting to strike.

While these animals can easily kill, none will go out of their way to prey on humans unless provoked. Therefore as writers, we *must* familiarise ourselves with the natural characteristics of any animal we wish to use in our novel. We need to know how they hunt and kill their prey; how they move, sleep and eat – and there *must* be a plausible reason why they are acting in a manner alien to normal behaviour. The horror is in the reaction to abnormal behaviour, and if this is a result of some human inter-ference with the habitat, there *must* be convincing scientific reasons why this mutation has occurred. The real terror stems from human agency altering the balance between the species as reflected in *Animal Kingdom: An Apocalyptic Horror Novel* (2011) by Iain Rob Wright.

Peter Benchley didn't credit his great white shark in *Jaws* with any super-intelligence, and although it often appears to be blessed with innate cunning, it was its sheer size and strength that made it so terrifying and deadly. The shark was merely doing what sharks do – but on a much grander scale! Similarly, in *The Deep* (1976), he uses the irascible temperament of a conga eel to thwart the pursuit of a villain! The screenplay written by Duncan Kennedy for the science fiction horror film, *Deep Blue Sea*, has a team of medics violating a code of ethics in extracting brain tissue from captive sharks – a process that makes them 'smarter, faster and more dangerous'.

Terror is the dread of the use of systematic violence; horror the

dread of something unpredictable, soothing, that may have a potential for violence.

Session 6: Summary

Because this is probably a first novel, it is advisable to complete the typescript before approaching a publisher or agent, simply because these days few are willing to work with a new novelist on the basis of a synopsis and sample chapters. Writing a novel always takes much longer than planned, especially when there are other aspects of life to get in the way, and you need to be in a position to come up with the goods if a publisher likes what he sees. If there are still months of work before the typescript is finished, the offer might be withdrawn if the publisher has to wait — or the commissioning editor moves on to another company.

In an article published in *The Author,* the quarterly journal of the Society of Authors, a commissioning editor admitted that if she wasn't sold on an idea in five minutes, then the proposal was rejected because this was the length of time *she* had to sell the idea at the monthly commissioning meeting. This is why it is essential to make every word count and why a great deal of time and effort should be made when putting together your proposal. Even online publishing companies require a 'full package' and a decision to offer a contract will probably be made on the strength of three readers' reports alone.

For the purpose of this exercise, prepare a covering letter, author biography, synopsis and two sample chapters – even if there is still a long way to go before the novel is actually finished and ready to go – because it's an exercise that might just tip the balance in your favour when the time comes. Don't forget that publishing is a different world now and you'll need to be aware of how each publisher requires submissions to be made. Check on the website for submission details, and follow these to the letter if you want them to take your inquiry/submission seriously.

For an insight into finding a publisher, particularly online publishers, it might be a good idea to invest in *The Author's Guide to Publishing and Marketing* (Compass Books) by Tim Ward and John Hunt at this stage and read it thoroughly before your proposal is ready to be sent.

The Covering Letter

Keep it sharp and concise. Do not include details impertinent to the novel since your contribution to the parish magazine doesn't interest a professional editor ... unless the plot revolves around such a scenario. Do include any professional writing credits or regular column commitments as this gives the indication that you are able to work within a team framework. Identify your target market and show how your book differs from other novels already published. Publishers will expect you to do a certain amount of marketing to promote your book, so show that you are fully conversant with the market for your own genre.

The Author Biography

Write a short paragraph on how you would like to see yourself described on the back cover of the book. Be sharp and concise, listing any previous titles and publishing credits. For example for this book I've said:

Suzanne Ruthven is a former member of the now late lamented Gothic Society, a regular contributor to its magazine *Udolpho* during its lifetime, and author of the horror novel, *Whittlewood*. On a more respectable level she is commissioning editor for Compass Books, the writers' resource imprint for John Hunt Publishing. Her latest offering in the horror genre is *House of Strange Gods*, due for publication in 2014.

This tells the reader all they need to know – that the writer is a professional within the publishing industry, and familiar with the horror genre; has been regularly published in a Gothic literary magazine; published a horror novel and currently working on another. Everything here is pertinent to the specific title being submitted for consideration.

The Synopsis

Any successful author will tell you that preparing a synopsis is almost as difficult as writing the whole damned book! It's the ultimate test in editing skills and every word must count in terms of conveying an overview of both plot and characters. For such an important element of the creative writing process, however, there are no 'carved in stone' guidelines as to the correct length of the thing, and an individual editor's requirements can differ quite considerably. As can the instructions given in the various how-to books.

In *The Writers' Guide to Getting Published,* Chriss McCallum gives the following advice, which is pretty standard throughout the industry. She tells us to send:

A concise synopsis of the whole novel, written in the present tense. Touch on key scenes, making it clear who is your main character, what their ultimate goal is, who and what stands between them and that goal. Show how the story ends. New writers often try to conceal the ending in an attempt to intrigue. This is a big mistake. The agent or editor needs to be able to assess the story as a whole.

Generally speaking, the synopsis should be no longer than one A4 page and *single* spaced, although it is not uncommon for some to be anything from 5-10 pages! Keep it short, sharp and concise; make every word count and spend some time in getting it right. Don't leave it until the last minute. In fact, think of it as a job application and give it your best shot.

Ask yourself: 'Would this tempt me into buying the book?' If in doubt ask someone else.

The Sample Chapters

The sample should consist of the first two chapters, not a random selection from the middle of the book. It is not uncommon for a publisher to receive chapters 35 and 54 with the explanation that these are considered to be the best example of the writer's work! As we've said before, the horror story must hook the attention from the first page and if it doesn't, no one is going to bother turning to page 2. Everything hinges on that opening but once hooked, the reader will, hopefully, go on to judge your writing style and story-telling ability.

Make sure that the presentation is crisp and readable (no fading ink cartridges), double-spaced and runs to approx 50 pages in order to give a fair representation of the plot/storyline. Attach a cover sheet stating title, author's name contact details, together with a word count.

Online publishers usually have a link on the website for submitting inquiries and proposals, so make sure you have everything ready to go. If submitting by post, check on the commissioning editor's name and address the letter to them personally. This shows you've not merely stuck a pin in the *Writer's Handbook* or *Writers' & Artists' Yearbook,* although both reference books give good advice on the preferred method of approach for each publishing house or agent ... ignore this at your peril. Bear in mind that personnel change, so phone the switchboard and ask for the name of the editor in charge of horror fiction.

Publishers and Agents

Hopefully, all the time you've been working on your typescript, you'll have been keeping an eye on who's publishing your particular brand of horror, and will have a good idea of who's going to be the recipient of your prized baby. Again, there is little point leaving this until the last minute ... successful authors should know as much about the marketplace as they do about writing.

It's often been said that it takes twice as long to sell a piece of writing as it does to write it. The road to publication is a long one and fraught with disappointments and pitfalls and it helps to understand a little of what goes on behind the scenes. Remember that an agent doesn't receive a penny until your book has been sold and fewer are taking on new writers, simply because the time and effort spent trying to market the typescript may be more than it's worth in terms of commission. You may be pleased with an offer of a £2,000 advance but the agent will have only earned £200, which may not cover the expense of selling it. And many smaller publishers pay no advance at all.

Whilst it is now generally considered permissible to simultaneously submit your typescript to several publishers, it is not considered good form to try to hook more than one agent at a time. They *do* talk to each other and will not be best pleased to find that you've been dealing with a competitor. Both agents and publishers are notoriously slow in getting back to the author, who is nervously chewing their fingernails and anxiously waiting for a reply. So how long do we give them to respond?

Providing you've enclosed the relevant postage, and/or a contact email address, they should manage to make some sort of response within a month. If you haven't heard back within that time, send the typescript off to the next one on your list. Some publishers state they don't want to receive simultaneous submissions and this is fine if they get back to you by return. One writer of our acquaintance has been waiting over a year for a reply, having been asked to submit the full typescript and does not want to jeopardise her chances by sending it to someone else. Personally, I wouldn't have given it six weeks – but then this is where personal choice comes into the equation.

Starting on the Next One

Once you've finished your novel and it's been submitted to the publisher/agent, you should already be thinking about the next one. Publishers like to think you've got something else in the pipeline because these days they are not interested in one-off novelists, so make sure you mention Number Two in your covering letter, even if it's just in the planning stages and you only have a 'working title'.

Be prepared for the second novel being more difficult to write than the first. This is probably because you will have temporarily emptied your store of spontaneous creativity. Don't worry, it will come back if you use the same formula for plotting but you may have to work a little harder to come up with new thoughts rather than simply rehashing ideas from your first book.

What Next?

When you have completed this final exercise, assess the results to see if you can spot any flaws, omissions or weaknesses, and whether you feel that the submission would be likely to attract positive attention. We should already be looking at the novel from a publisher's, or agent's viewpoint, and have a good idea of whether it has *commercial,* rather than literary merit. Don't worry if your novel is nowhere near finished because these are just exercises to get you thinking along the right lines for the future. Just because it *is* an exercise, however, don't skimp on the trial-run submission package – give it everything you've got!

Exercise – Session 6: Summary

1 Prepare a synopsis and author biography as per the brief given above. And take your time – this is an important part of the submission process.
2 Prepare the revised first and second opening chapters.
3 Prepare a covering letter that includes any information

pertinent to the novel submission.

4 Make notes of where you will be sending your novel, either direct to a publisher or via a literary agent. And list your reasons for selecting this route.

5 Have you made any notes for a second novel at this stage? If so, is it a fresh idea, or will you be attempting to breathe new life into an old one?

Cosmic Egg publisher's interview

Suzanne Ruthven former member of The Gothic Society, talks to Krystina Kellingley, publisher of Cosmic Egg, a new imprint of John Hunt Publishing specialising in science fiction, fantasy and horror novels that offers excellent opportunities for new writes.

SR: Although horror novels have always been seen as the poor relation in the literary stakes, in reality the standard of writing by the original authors in the genre was extremely high. Do you continue to set these high standards for would-be Cosmic Egg authors?

KK: The horror market is an extremely competitive and difficult market to break into, so any aspiring author has to present high quality work. However, if a story has great potential we will work with an author to iron out any problems with the manuscript.

SR: As a guideline on your Blog 'How To Write A Novel' you state that essentially the bones of any horror story is the eternal struggle between good and evil. The author's task is to set this against a new backdrop. Would you like to expand on this advice?

KK: Just as there are no entirely new plots in any genre, there is also nothing that hasn't been written about in the horror sector. Having said that, horror/fantasy is growing in popularity so authors are continuing to find new stories to tell. The only way to do that is to find a different angle. You can achieve this through setting your story on a different world or in a different time period or by making your characters so compelling that the reader is driven by the need to know their personal story and their fate. Another way is to mix horror and fantasy, something which has worked very well for Steven King, Robert McCammon and Robert Jordan to name just a few.

SR: What exciting titles do you have in the pipeline and why did you select these as your first publications?

KK: We have some great titles in production to suit all tastes. 'Orders From Above' by JM Forrest, centres around an agreement made between Lucifer and Gabriel. It's very funny and sharp, a great read. In complete contrast, 'Gem's Story' is quite a spiritual and uplifting tale. 'Eladria' is an exciting, fast paced combination of fantasy and sci-fi with great characters and plot, guaranteed to keep you turning pages and 'Wellsprings' is a wonderful story of what happens in a world where the ecosystem has broken down under human abuse. Last but certainly not least is 'Wooing the Echo', the first of the Christopher Penrose Novels. This one is an occult tale of magic, other dimensions and a lonely vampire.

I chose these titles for two reasons. Firstly because I enjoyed reading them enough to become invested in them and secondly because they are well written and I'm proud to have the authors represent Cosmic Egg.

SR: Do you accept traditional Gothic horror, or are you looking for more contemporary material?

KK: I'm happy to accept any type of horror as long as it is well written with a strong plot and three-dimensional characters.

SR: Judging from the hints on your Blog, you like stories that are character-led, with plenty of strong personalities to drive the narrative along. Is there anything you'd like to add?

KK: There's no magic ingredient that I can point to as a recipe for success. The old adage about writing being 10 per cent inspiration and 90 per cent perspiration holds true. A writer has to be prepared to write, edit, re-write and hone material until it feels ready. If you're not quite certain that it works then don't send it. Re-read and edit again as necessary. If you're not convinced then it's unlikely anyone else will be.

SR: What other hints do you have for authors wanting to write for you?

KK: Do your research – Read good authors who are writing the type of book you want to write. Get the facts straight. Make sure you know your mythology/demonology or any other information you may want to include in your writing. Before you present your manuscript make sure you have your grammar, speech and narrative polished. If you can get someone to read it before presenting it, so much the better. If not, at least put it aside for a while after it is finished before re-appraising it. Sometimes writing requires a sacrifice – never be afraid to kill off your 'babies'. You may love that phrase or that idea but if it adds nothing to the story you need to lose it. Very importantly check the layout; have you set out the speech correctly? Have you used single quote marks for the UK and double quotes if it's USA? Have you mixed one character's speech with another character's actions or thoughts?

SR: How should potential authors contact you in the first instance?

KK: Authors need to apply through the site, http://www.cosmicegg-books.com and follow the instructions. Good luck!

Conclusion

We are repeatedly informed that horror is out of fashion, and then along comes another new author like Iain Rob Wright or Bentley Little to inject fresh blood into the genre – and all the old classics get a new lease of life – to sit alongside perennial favourites like Stephen King and Robert R McCammon. The truth of the matter is that exciting horror fiction always had its aficionados, and good writing will always attract a loyal following.

One of the best writing tools available for would-be authors in the genre is Amazon's Listmania, compiled by avid readers of horror fiction and offering a unique guide to the most popular books and authors. For example, the following selection of top horror novels was compiled by horror writer Isaac LeFevre at the time of going to press, but for up to date listings go to www.amazon.com/horrorfiction and study the customer reviews to see what was liked – and what wasn't – about the different titles.

Ghost Story by Peter Straub (157 customer reviews)
Usher's Passing by Robert R McCammon (42 customer reviews)
Swan Song by Robert R McCammon (801 customer reviews)
I Am Legend by Richard Matheson (812 customer reviews)
Walkers by Graham Masterton (17 customer reviews)
The Shining by Stephen King (853 customer reviews)
Pet Sematary by Stephen King (488 customer reviews)
The Store by Bentley Little (136 customer reviews)
Phantoms by Dean Koontz (292 customer reviews)
Ghosts by Noel Hynd (76 customer reviews)
Boy's Life by Robert R McCammonn (353 customer reviews)
Spirit by Graham Masterton (18 customer reviews)

The House that Jack Built by Graham Masterton (42 customer reviews)

The Association by Bentley Little (137 customer reviews)

Remember these are the viewpoints of the reading public who regularly buy horror novels, and whom you will ultimately be writing for when you start to create your story. The listings also throw up the small, independent publishers that specialise in horror fiction, and who do not usually appear on mainstream (i.e. corporate) publishers' listings. Time spent investigating this area of books already in the marketplace could provide a valuable insight into the world of authors and publishers. Although it is important to be familiar with the classics of the genre, it is also important to be on 'reading terms' with more contemporary titles and authors.

On Amazon, veteran Guy N Smith's author biography concludes with the words: "My readership has remained faithful to me and technology has made it all possible again with e-books. Thus my backlist is steadily returning to electronic print along with some new books. It is an exciting time."

I couldn't agree more.

COMPASS BOOKS

Compass Books focuses on practical and informative 'how-to' books for writers. Written by experienced authors who also have extensive experience of tutoring at the most popular creative writing workshops, the books offer an insight into the more specialised niches of the publishing game.

9781782792666